THE GARDENS OF
WILLIAM MORRIS

THE GARDENS OF
WILLIAM MORRIS

JILL DUCHESS OF HAMILTON,
PENNY HART & JOHN SIMMONS

Foreword by Sir Roy Strong

FRANCES LINCOLN

Dedicated to Mavis Batey, President of the Garden
History Society, who, like William Morris, has done
so much to preserve the architectural and garden
heritage of England. She shares his ideal that:
'We are only trustees for those that come after us.'

Flora-for-Fauna, registered charity no. 1060715

Frances Lincoln Limited
4 Torriano Mews
Torriano Avenue
London NW5 2RZ
www.franceslincoln.com

British Library Cataloguing-in-Publication data
A catalogue record for this book is available from the British Library.

ISBN 10: 0-7112-2609-1
ISBN 13: 978-0-7112-2609-8

Set in Berling Roman
Printed in Singapore

Half title page: Kelmscott Manor, Oxfordshire: the front entrance.
*Frontispiece: The Red House, Bexleyheath: a glimpse of the well-house
through leaded glass.*
*Contents page: William Morris (seated) with Edward Burne-Jones in the
garden of The Grange, Fulham, in the 1890s.*

1 3 5 7 9 8 6 4 2

CONTENTS

Painting by Marie Stillman of Kelmscott Manor, home of the Morris family from 1871 and where William Morris created a garden. He is well known as the main inspiration of the Arts and Crafts movement but his influence on gardens is often overlooked.

His ideal garden had straight paths and beds filled with an abundance of old-fashioned flowers. At Kelmscott he used hedges to contrast with the free-flowing masses of plants and flowers in the herbaceous borders.

FOREWORD

Before you become beguiled by the beauty of this book and embark on the voyage into William Morris's garden dreamland, I want to tell you about the garden experience from the last couple of years that sticks most in my mind. It took place in the Netherlands. Two young men had created a quite extraordinary garden. Modest in scale, as virtually all Dutch gardens are, it consisted of a series of enclosures and included a number of surprising features, like a long border of poisonous plants that we were bidden not to touch. One area, I noticed, had the entrance firmly barred against intruders. As I poked my head over the closed gate, trying to catch a glimpse of what lay hidden within, I wondered what secrets it held. Then one of my hosts said he would like to show it to me as a special privilege, one which had so far been accorded only to Beth Chatto. With that honour bestowed, I felt that I was about to be admitted to paradise.

Entering by way of what was in effect a field hedge, I found myself in a small enclosure with a pond at its heart, the earth to make it having been scooped out and banked up around the sides. At one end of the patch of water an observation pit had been sunk, signalling that I had entered a garden dedicated to nature unpolluted. I was indeed embowered within a haze of wild flowers and grasses, field hedge trees and plants, the water's edge laced with wild irises and marsh marigolds. The pond was a sanctuary for frogs and toads and, above its surface, dragonflies hovered while butterflies flitted past me. William Morris would have felt very much at home here. I was then taken to the far side of the enclosure and invited to look out at the landscape beyond. Before my eyes stretched a flat tract of bare earth. 'Now we must take into our gardens and grow what our farmers have destroyed,' said my host. Returning to 'paradise', he told me that all the plants in his garden were indigenous to that area of the Low Countries. They had once been commonplace. Now they are endangered species.

Take that little story of mine to heart, for it is this volume's central message. *The Gardens of William Morris* is not comfort reading but a tract for the times, applicable to every small patch of earth that any reader is fortunate enough to have as a garden. The mission statement is a simple one. Always make room for one or more species that are native to the island, and in particular your area of it, and so help preserve our threatened plant heritage. And secondly, go organic. Make a firm resolution never to spray or use any form of chemicals. Rather, let the weeds grow, remembering that they too can be beautiful, and welcome in the glorious waves of wildlife that will come your way. You will never regret it.

Roy Strong

THE VERY MAKING OF
A HOMESTEAD

As THE GREATEST TEXTILE DESIGNER of the Victorian era, William Morris is usually associated with interiors: fabrics, wallpapers and carpets. Yet he was equally, if not more, concerned with the exteriors of buildings and their surroundings. Forging a union with nature and the past was his ambition, and it extended well beyond the house. Morris's love of nature was one of his ruling passions – and perhaps his most sublime. Trees, flowers, birds and rivers were a source of inspiration and a well-spring of his work. Just as he transferred petals, leaves and curling stems to the interior walls and windows of houses, so he took the concept of the 'rooms' of a house outside into the garden. There was a continuous cross-fertilization between the plants and birds on his drawing board and those flourishing in his gardens. Applying to the garden his principles – harmony with nature and homage to tradition – he strove to combine the old with the new, the formal with the wild, order with exuberance. His perfect garden was as rhythmical and structured as his textile patterns.

Always mindful of the distinctive natural character of a place, he fought against the spread of unthinking uniformity. In his 1880 lecture 'The Prospects of Architecture', Morris said that each new house had taken away 'a little piece of the flowery green sward, a few yards of the teeming hedge-row'. He urged his audience to remember the original plant cover before it was replaced with houses:

> the earth which was beautiful before man lived on it, which for many ages grew in beauty as men grew in numbers and power, is now growing uglier day by day, and there the swiftest where civilisation is the mightiest . . . as we . . . see the arid and pretentious little gardens, and cast-iron horrors of railings, and miseries of squalid outhouses breaking through the sweet meadows and abundant hedge-rows of our old quiet hamlet, do not our hearts sink within us . . .

Art pays homage to nature in Jane Morris's embroidery of apple blossom, echoed by the froth of real flowers on an apple tree seen through a window at the Red House. During the five happy years the Morrises spent there, Jane would often sit stitching in the garden.

In *The Quest*, the magazine of the Birmingham Guild of Handicraft, he wrote in 1895: 'Many a good house both old and new is marred by the vulgarity and stupidity of its garden, so that one is tormented by having to abstract in one's mind the good building from the nightmare of "horticulture" which surrounds it.' A garden, he went on to say, 'is often the very making of a homestead . . . in great towns, gardens, both private and public, are positive necessities if the citizens are to live reasonable and healthy lives in body and mind'.

A continuing thread throughout Morris's artistic work is the indigenous flora. Local plants such as violets, fritillaries and willows are woven into intricate patterns, sometimes as a centrepiece, sometimes half-hidden. Blackbirds feast on wild strawberries (*Strawberry Thief* fabric), honeysuckle tangles with yew twigs (*Woodpecker* tapestry), wild roses clamber through a trellis (*Trellis* wallpaper). Exuberant designs interweave indigenous plants and imported varieties: native daisies with exotic sunflowers, English dog-roses beside a stately lily, honeysuckle with a grand crown imperial. Flowers of meadow and stream appear in Morris's wallpapers, textiles, tapestries, carpets, stained glass and book designs. Together with gardens and trees they are glorified in his verse and lauded in his lectures and prose.

Morris's ideal garden contained the essence of the man and his history. From his boyhood reading came chivalric scenes and romantic images of knights and their ladies in vine-covered bowers. From studying Gerard's sixteenth-century *Herball* with its woodblock drawings of plants, he retained the picture of an early garden, all cruciform paths and neat, raised beds. Like his favourite childhood author, Sir Walter Scott, Morris felt that 'nothing is more the Child of Art than a garden'.

He and his friends the Pre-Raphaelite painters were stirred by the vigorous simplicity of an older, pre-industrial England. It was the England of the Middle Ages that shaped his radical approach to art. It also formed his attitude to horticulture. True to his maxim of 'beauty and utility', he admired the practicalities of medieval gardens, with their shady arbours and their sensible combination of fruit trees, vegetables, herbs and flowers. The

*ABOVE A trellised garden with flowery mead in an illustration
from the fifteenth-century* Roman de la Rose *by Guillaume de la
Lorris and* LEFT *a rose trellis in this scene from the early French*
Poems of Christine de Pisan *resemble those designed
by Morris for the Red House garden.*

OPPOSITE *Morris's* Woodpecker *tapestry, 1885, illustrates the interdependence of plants and animals that recurs throughout his work.*

garden as a place of mystery and repose was central to Morris's imagination.

Morris used the past as a tutor for the present, creating a new world on the best traditions of the old: 'the greatest side of art is the art of daily life which historical buildings represent . . . for making the past part of the present . . .' He liked to imagine that the towns of the future would grow out of the soil they stood on. But most of all he wanted to 'turn this land from the grimy back-yard of a workshop into a garden'. According to his rule, suburban houses, each with their own patch of greenery, would form leafy buffer-zones between town and country: 'And at last the suburb proper, mostly fields and fruit gardens with scanty houses dotted about till you come to the open country.'

Although Morris's original gardens have faded, his ideas were absorbed by other designers who transformed English gardens in ways that became admired and imitated throughout the world. Fiona MacCarthy, in her influential biography of Morris, goes so far as to declare that the first Victorian example of square plot and trained hedge garden was at the Red House, Morris's first marital home (see page 39). She adds, 'Morris's insistence on the integration of the garden and the building encouraged a new movement in English garden design . . . Without Morris in fact would there have been a Gertrude Jekyll?'

Morris never wrote a treatise on gardening, nor did he work as a professional garden designer. But his thoughts and opinions emerge again and again in his novels, poetry and, perhaps above all, in his letters. The picture of William Morris's ideal garden becomes clear when these are combined with his series of lectures, published in 1882 as *Hopes and Fears for Art*, which stress the importance of gardens, inveighing against pollution and the urbanization of the countryside. His gardening principles were taken up by the Arts and Crafts movement and through its followers went on to influence a successive generation of garden designers.

THE PRINCIPLES OF MORRIS'S GARDEN DESIGN

MORRIS'S PRINCIPLES ON DESIGN and plant heritage are as valid now as they were in the late nineteenth century. He strove for a perfect synthesis of the natural and the formal, of old-fashioned plants and new introductions. He favoured flowing planting in a structured setting, using brick, stone, wattle and wood. His search to find renewal in industrial England by using traditional materials and local plants is now paralleled by the urge in an increasingly urban country to create gardens more in sympathy with nature. The revival of interest in the countryside, added to an increasing concern for wildlife, should take Morris's gardening ideas well into the millennium.

UNIFY HOUSE AND GARDEN

To Morris, a home was one of the most significant features in anyone's life: 'If I were asked to say what is at once the most important production of Art and the thing most to be longed for I should answer: a beautiful House . . .' Gardens, he believed, should 'clothe' the building – acting as a floral extension to link the house with the surrounding country. As he wrote in *The Quest*, 'The garden, divided by old clipped yew hedges, is quite unaffected and very pleasant, and looks in fact as if it were a part of the house, yet at least the clothes of it: which I think ought to be the aim of the layer-out of a garden.'

Although Morris promoted this concept of bringing gardens closer to the house, the idea of trellised enclosures for flowers near the house, in contrast to sweeping parkland beyond, had already been mooted by the great landscape gardener, Humphry Repton. Morris begged gardeners of the day not to follow blindly the latest horticultural fashion and try to tease their small plots into imitation landscapes. Harrumphed Morris:

In this cartoon of 1862 for stained glass at Harden Grange, near Bingley in Yorkshire, Morris himself is the model for King Arthur, seen with the knight Lancelot. The wattle fence is similar to that found in medieval manuscripts – and to those used by Morris at the Red House and at Kelmscott Manor. The king's robe is patterned with bright sunflowers and daisies grow at their feet.

our suburban gardeners in London, for instance, oftenest wind about their little bit of gravel walk and grass plot in ridiculous imitation of an ugly big garden of the landscape-gardening style, and then with a strange perversity fill up the spaces with the most formal plants they can get; whereas the merest common sense should have taught them to lay out their morsel of ground in the simplest way, to fence it as orderly as might be, one part from the other (if it be big enough for that) and the whole from the road.

ENCLOSE THE GARDEN WITH TREES, HEDGES OR NATURAL-LOOKING FENCES

Morris's model garden looked back to the medieval *hortus conclusus*, a symmetrical structure of local materials, enclosed by hedges and trees, with straight paths and beds softened by an abundance of cottage-garden flowers. Strange as it may seem now, Morris's garden, although drawn from the past, was avant-garde and almost shocking in the 1860s. Over 25 years later it was still sufficiently new and interesting to feature in his lecture 'Making the Best of It' (1879), in which he said:

Large or small, [the garden] should look both orderly and rich. It should be well fenced from the outside world. It should by no means imitate either the wilfulness or wildness of Nature, but should look like a thing never to be seen except near a house. It should in fact look like part of a house. It follows from this that no private-pleasure garden should be very big, and a public garden should be divided and made to look like so many flower-closes in a meadow, or a wood, or amidst the pavement.

In other words, Morris believed that the garden should be a series of 'rooms', with hedges, wattle fences and trees as the 'walls', giving a sense of privacy, furnished with the straight lines of paths and borders, and decorated with an exuberance of flowers. What is more, the wattle fences should be made of local willow and hazel, as they were in his gardens at the Red House and Kelmscott Manor.

PRESERVE LOCAL IDENTITY

Morris saw that as the world became ever more homogeneous, so the need to establish local identity grew. Place names, languages, dialects, food, beer, architecture and pride in landscape – all were, and still are, increasingly precious. In the same way, the very heart of a place, the regional flora, was vitally important.

Morris thoroughly disliked Palladian mansions set in parks, because they had no connection or continuity with the area; he preferred structures – whether stone, fences, barns or buildings – that had evolved from the traditions of a district. As one of the early advocates of the use of the vernacular, he reaffirmed pride in regional identity, using local materials: bricks made from clay

dug in the vicinity; stone from the neighbourhood; fences and floors from nearby trees. When alterations were made to his country house at Kelmscott, every nail was fashioned by the village smith, the stone for window repairs came from local quarries, and the roof and dado were made from local elms.

Morris insisted on traditional wood and stone for the hard landscaping to integrate the garden with its surroundings. He had a deep understanding of the handling of materials and their possibilities. He disliked iron fencing: 'when you fence anything in a garden use a live hedge, or stones set flatwise (as they do in some parts of the Cotswold country), or timber, or wattle, or, in short, anything but iron.'

A drawing of Kelmscott Manor showing Morris's garden. Each area or 'room' is separated by hedges, wattle fences or vine-covered walls. Each has a distinct layout and different plants, although all share symmetry and straight hedges – intended to make a satisfying contrast with the mass of untamed flowers.

Morris never ceased to remind people of the value of indigenous materials. In a lecture to farm workers (at Buscot, near Kelmscott), Morris called on them to appreciate their ancient stone buildings. On another occasion he wrote to the Thames Conservancy Board concerning a proposal to rebuild a lock-keeper's cottage near Kelmscott, stressing that one of the most characteristic features of the neighbourhood was the prevalence of old houses built of local stone:

> . . . and roofed with stone – slates or slabs: and I have noticed that any intrusion of other materials materially injures the landscape. This would be certainly the case if a building of red brick covered with ordinary slate took the place of the present cottage.

His special loathing was for classical and picturesque houses with their artificially created landscapes, idealized vistas and romantic ruins. He went so far as to dismiss the grand landscaped gardens of the day as 'barren classicalism'. Morris saw these houses and gardens as a sham. He felt they had no legitimacy, having been born neither of English history nor of English nature.

Morris's aim was to promote the beauty of familiar places, and, above all, the regional flora. According to his biographer, Professor Paul Thompson, Morris's textile designs had 'led the return to British flowers, many wild from the country hedges, in parallel with the rise of the partly wilder, flower-filled garden, reflecting the changing seasons rather than the efficiency of the greenhouse'. At a time when Victorian gardeners were obsessed with imported exotics, elaborate hybrids and regiments of garish bedding plants, this was revolutionary. Indigenous plants are not flamboyant, but they have a natural, quiet charm of their own that Morris recognized.

On a wider scale he was among the first to campaign effectively against destruction of the environment, fighting to prevent damage to Britain's forests and the felling of trees – the core of ancient landscapes: 'I very much fear that the intention of the authorities is to clear the forest of its native trees and to plant vile weeds like deodars and outlandish conifers instead,' protested Morris in a letter to the *Daily Chronicle* in 1895. He also railed against the neglect of England's riverbank flora, on the same occasion, asking the Thames Conservancy Board to instruct their workmen to spare the native flowers when cutting weeds on the river banks.

PLANT SIMPLE FLOWERS

Morris expressed his love of simple flowers in a letter to his family: 'snowdrops are everywhere . . . they give a delightful idea of spring about: there are a few violets out and here and there a coloured primrose . . . how pretty it looks to see the promise of things pushing up through the clean un-sooty soil.' For Morris, the root of art was in 'nature': 'I must have unmistakable suggestions of gardens and fields, and strange trees, boughs and tendrils, or I can't do with your pattern,' he said when lecturing on design. Again: 'All works of man that we live amongst and handle will be in harmony with nature.'

By advocating a profusion of simple plants, he demonstrated how he adapted – not copied – the practices of the past. In the medieval gardens that so influenced him, flowers were sparse. But in his lecture 'Making the Best of It', he urged gardeners:

> to fill up the flower-growing space with things that are free and interesting in their growth, leaving Nature to do the desired complexity, which she will certainly not fail to do if we do not desert her for the florist, who, I must say has made it harder work than it should be to get the best of flowers.

The word 'florist' in Morris's time was used to describe breeders who crossed flowers to increase the size or number of the petals, often converting them into showy doubles. Morris's refined senses were offended by the artificiality of the new cultivars and he contemptuously referred to them as 'florist flowers'. Morris cherished natural flowers and deplored such manipulation of plants and the consequent flood of over-developed blooms – in his words: 'change without thought of beauty, change for the sake of change'.

15

Morris was particularly upset by the constant meddling with one of his favourite flowers, the rose, until it had been bred to the size of a cabbage, with an artificial smell and colour. To him, the wild rose could not be improved upon: 'nothing can be more beautiful in general growth or in detail than a wayside bush of it, nor can any scent be as sweet and pure as its scent.' He was distressed, too, by the doubling of the imported sunflower from Mexico. In one of his lectures published as 'Hopes and Fears for Art', he instructed his audience:

> Be very shy of double flowers; choose the old columbine where the clustering doves are unmistakable and distinct, not the double one, where they run into tatters. . . Choose (if you can get it) the old china-aster with the yellow centre . . . Don't be swindled out of that wonder of beauty, a single snowdrop; there is no gain and plenty of loss in the double one . . .

Morris's observation that simple flowers attract bees and butterflies was proved recently at Cambridge University Botanic Garden. Experiments show that single flowers are a valuable source of nectar for insects, whereas many modern cultivars provide meagre fare. Some of the new flowers have little or no nectar; others produce nectar but insects cannot reach it – they are obstructed by double petals or 'improvements' in the bloom. Increasing the number and size of the petals and brightening the colours is, alas, often at the price of altered sexual organs and sometimes sterility.

ESCHEW FASHION

Among the displays of wealth of the new rich of the industrial era were gardens packed with assortments of horticultural freaks. Some unfortunate exotic plants had been selected simply for their bizarre appearance, like alien creatures in a zoo, and these Morris condemned as

> plants which are curiosities only, which Nature meant to be grotesque, not beautiful, and which are generally the growth of hot countries where things sprout over-quick and rank. Take note that the strangest of these come from the jungle and the tropical waste, from places where man is not at home, but is an intruder, an enemy. Go to a botanical garden and look at

them, and think of those strange places to your heart's content. But don't set them to starve in your smoke-drenched scrap of ground amongst the bricks, for they will be no ornament to it.

Plant-hunters and sea captains had introduced thousands of half-hardy plants from all over the world, including lobelias, calceolarias, antirrhinums, ageratum, petunias and begonias. Large-scale sales of plants hitherto unsuitable for British winters were made possible by the 1845 lifting of the glass tax which allowed huge commercial hothouses to be built. In addition, every British household of any pretension had at least one greenhouse and a conservatory. Cheap light and heat meant that vast numbers of tropical plants could now survive. This floral explosion, coupled with the development of plant breeding skills, meant that nineteenth-century gardeners had a wide choice of plants – by 1830 there were 1,500 varieties of dahlia.

Many of these new varieties were used in the Victorian craze for 'bedding-out' – the tight massing of annually produced tender plants – and 'carpet bedding' – the making of intricate patterns with low-growing coloured foliage plants. Some were set out in geometrically shaped flower beds. The combination of gaudy plants and elaborate settings enraged the notoriously short-fused Morris, who denounced the fashion as

> an aberration of the human mind which otherwise I should have been ashamed to warn you of. It is technically called carpet-bedding. Need I explain further? I had rather not, for when I think of it even, when I am quite alone, I blush with shame at the thought.

Morris's censure, so powerfully expressed, was taken up by his contemporary, William Robinson, in *The English Flower Garden* (see page 87).

> *Sunflower, wallpaper, 1879. Sunflowers were among Morris's favourite plants, appearing in his designs and in his prose and lectures. He warned against cross-breeding to make showier blooms: 'the double sunflower . . . is a coarse-coloured and dull plant, whereas the single one . . . is both interesting and beautiful, with its sharply chiselled yellow florets relieved by the quaintly patterned sad-coloured centre clogged with honey and beset with bees and butterflies.'*

Columbine, printed cotton, 1876 (trial printing). The design, thought to be based on a fifteenth-century Rhenish linen, features the nodding heads of the single columbine preferred by Morris, and the delicate, pendulous flowers of the English bluebell that Morris so loved to see carpeting the woodland floor in spring.

So great was the enthusiasm for bedding-out that in London parks in the 1870s armies of gardeners grew two million plants each year solely for summer show. Sometimes this meant that for the remaining eight or nine months the soil was left unnaturally bare. These temporary plants could not reproduce in the temperate British climate, but they flowed from the glasshouse production line like the mass-manufactured goods that Morris hated. To Morris's fastidious eye, many popular plantings were the depths of bad taste. 'Flowers in masses are mighty strong colour, and if not used with a great deal of caution are very destructive to pleasure in gardening.' He hoped to turn the nineteenth-century bourgeoisie away from their obsession with bright new imports. In a letter to Mrs Alfred Baldwin, mother of the future Prime Minister, he spoke of his home as 'sweet and innocent' in comparison with modern villas with their displays of red geraniums. In 'Making the Best of It', he told his audience:

> On the whole, I think the best and safest plan is to mix up your flowers, and rather eschew great masses of colour – in combination I mean. But there are some flowers (inventions of men, i.e.: florists) which are bad colour altogether, and not to be used at all. Scarlet geraniums, for instance, or the yellow calceolaria, which indeed are not uncommonly grown together profusely, in order, I suppose to show that even flowers can be thoroughly ugly.

Equally favoured by the Victorian gardener and disliked by Morris were low-maintenance hardy evergreens for shrubberies. From China, Japan and the New World came rhododendron, camellia, spotted laurel, the monkey-puzzle tree and other conifers, which augmented and often replaced local deciduous trees and shrubs. In perpetual leaf, they hid the soil from the sun, so reducing the growth of ground flora, including spring flowers.

INTEGRATE EXISTING TREES

Trees in a garden were vital for Morris, not only to enhance the garden but to be seen from the windows of the house. In his lecture 'The Prospects of Architecture', he suggested that houses should be simply decorated with 'a sanded floor and whitewashed walls, and the green trees and flowery meads and living waters outside'.

As a conservationist, he was effective and far-sighted. He complained about the practice of developers pulling down old houses, then clearing sites of any existing trees. New houses should fit around the established trees (the Red House was built in this way); and builders should not 'begin by clearing a site till it is as bare as the pavement'. 'Making the Best of It' emphasized the point: 'in our part of the world few indeed have any mercy upon the one thing necessary for decent life in a town, its trees; till we have come to this, that . . . one trembles at the very sound of an axe as one sits at one's work at home.'

The hero of Morris's short story *A Dream of John Ball* (1886) laments the destruction of trees: 'On the other side of the water the few willow-trees left us by the Thames Conservancy looked doubtfully alive against the bleak sky . . .' In his epic poem published in 1868, *The Earthly Paradise*, Psyche finds herself in a wonderful country where:

> . . . all about were dotted leafy trees,
> The elm for shade, the linden for the bees
> . . . and in them hung
> Bright birds that elsewhere sing not, but here sung
> As sweetly as the small brown nightingales.

And Morris's dream of an abundance of trees is evident in his Utopian romance, *News from Nowhere* (1890):

> One change I noticed amidst the quiet beauty of the fields to wit, that they were planted with trees here and there, often fruit-trees, and that there was none of the niggardly begrudging of space to a handsome tree which I remembered too well; and though the willows were often polled (or shrowded [sic], as they call it in the countryside), this was done with some regard to beauty: I mean that there was no polling of rows on rows so as to destroy the pleasantness of half a mile of country, but a

19

thoughtful sequence in the cutting, that prevented a bareness anywhere. To be short, the fields were everywhere treated as a garden made for the pleasure as well as the livelihood of all.

Indeed, Morris seized every opportunity to protest actively against excessive tree cutting. The felling of hornbeams in his beloved Epping Forest provoked two letters to the *Daily Chronicle* in 1895: 'The special character of it [Epping Forest] was derived from the fact that by far the greater part was a wood of hornbeams. . . And I submit that no treatment of it can be tolerable which does not leave this hornbeam wood intact.'

MAKE IT PRODUCTIVE

Morris's gardens were functional spaces – people ate from them, relaxed in them, played in them. A garden, in his view, had to produce food for the household. Over and over again in Morris's poetry there are references to paradise gardens with fruit trees, especially apple trees. In the 'Quest of Jason' the argonauts reach a palace:

> Well-set with fair fruit-bearing trees, and groves
> Of thick-leaved elms, all populous of doves. . .

And later in the same poem, he describes the Garden of the Hesperides in which:

> . . . mid-most there
> Grew a green tree, whose smooth grey boughs did bear
> Such fruit as never man elsewhere had seen,
> For 'twixt the sunlight and the shadow green
> Shone out fair apples of red gleaming gold.

Fruit trees are common emblems in his tapestries. The 1890 tapestry *The Orchard* features apple, orange and pear trees with allegorical female figures holding a scroll inscribed with words from a Morris poem:

> But here within our orchard close
> the guerdon of our labour shows.

Fresh produce from the garden regularly appeared on the table at Kelmscott Manor. In season there were cherries, strawberries, raspberries, gooseberries, apples and plums, as well as home-grown greens. Even the garden at the works at Merton Abbey (see page 75) had a large vegetable patch that supplied delicacies such as asparagus.

INCLUDE PLACES FOR RECREATION AND RELAXATION

For Morris a garden was a source of enjoyment and mental refreshment. His wife, Jane, and daughter, May, would sit in their various gardens, sewing and talking. At the Red House, there were deep porches with chairs and tables where people could relax, exchange ideas and eat. They fulfilled much the same function as covered verandas in warmer climates. On the west side of the house was a grass walk and a bowling alley for bowls and skittles, and the crack of croquet mallets could often be heard on the front lawn.

At Kelmscott House in Hammersmith (see page 67), the Morrises again used the lawn as an arena for games. It also saw at least one garden party, when Octavia Hill, the founder of the National Trust, held a gathering there for her staff.

RIGHT An ancient apple tree in bloom at the Red House evokes the paradise gardens that Morris refers to frequently in his poetry and prose – ideal gardens that were both beautiful and productive, providing fruit and vegetables for the table.

PREVIOUS PAGES With its fruit trees and low trellis fence The Orchard *or* The Seasons *tapestry, 1890, recalls the orchard at the Red House and the bluebells, forget-me-nots, daffodils, primroses and pansies that still grow wild there among the trees.*

THE MAN
AND
HIS GARDENS

MORRIS WAS A MAN OF CONTRADICTIONS, a complex character whose tensions appeared to find perfect release through the balance and harmony of his creative work. He was a rough-edged radical whose religious parents were respected members of the higher bourgeoisie; a dreamer who was intensely practical; ruggedly masculine, yet with a delicate sensitivity; a man so strong he could lift two heavy chairs while picking up a coal bucket with his teeth, yet with an inherited weakness of constitution; a man of the people who often preferred places to humankind; a socialist who was a successful manufacturer; a countryman who lived most of his life in town; a self-confessed unbeliever who made stained-glass windows for churches. Exceptionally reticent about his personal life, he was given to passionate outpourings in his poetry and speeches.

Although Morris's work might be considered the essence of Englishness, his paternal ancestors on both sides were Welsh. This Celtic strain may have accounted for his romantic imagination and his almost mystical attachment to the past. Among his mother Emma's family, a social notch above his father's, were some talented musicians and artists, including one singing canon at Worcester Cathedral and another at Westminster Abbey. His father, William Morris senior, moved from Worcester to London, where he became a prosperous bill broker in the City.

Kelmscott House, Morris's last home, at Hammersmith. Much of the garden remains, although Pig End has been obliterated by a major road. The basement houses the William Morris Society.

25

EARLY YEARS

WILLIAM, the eldest boy of nine surviving children, was born in 1834 at Elm House, Walthamstow, then a village close enough to the City of London for his father to travel daily to and from his office by coach. Before he was five, the stocky, restless boy showed a precocious interest in medieval fantasy and in botany. He claimed to have read all Sir Walter Scott's novels by the age of seven. One of his childhood joys was nearby Epping Forest. Later he wrote: 'When I was a boy and young man I knew it yard by yard.' It inspired his intense feeling for nature and he never ceased to love it, images of the forest appearing again and again in his poetry and prose romances. The young Morris walked every path in the woods, gazing awestruck at the tall poles of the pollarded hornbeams against the dark holly thickets. On horseback, he rode the lanes of Essex in search of churches and was affected by a visit to Queen Elizabeth's Lodge, near Chingford Hatch, where he had his 'first acquaintance [sic] with a room hung with faded greenery . . . and the impression of romance it made upon me!'

In 1840 the prosperous Morris family moved to Woodford Hall in Essex, an impressive Georgian house set in 50 acres of park on the edge of Epping Forest, which was separated from the grounds only by a fence. This eighteenth-century mansion was Morris's home from the age of six to fourteen, and it was here that he was able to indulge his interests, arranging his own garden, reading aloud to his favourite older sister, Emma, roaming alone on his pony, fishing and exploring the forest.

ABOVE *The earliest known photograph of Morris, taken when he was 23.*

LEFT *Epping Forest, where the young Morris acquired his intense feeling for nature.*

Morris acquired an intimate knowledge of the low-lying Essex countryside. The shapes of buildings on the horizon, the golden glow of marsh marigolds and the fine markings on a bird's plumage all excited his senses; so, too, did the sights and scents of his childhood garden. In adulthood, he could recall the exact form of a blue hepatica and the smell of may blossom wafting through his bedroom window.

Morris's father died at the age of 50, a few months before Morris went to the newly established Marlborough College in Wiltshire. But owing to an inspired investment in a Devon copper mine in 1845, Morris senior left the family rich and with a recently acquired coat of arms. In later years, Morris the socialist was uncomfortably conscious of his father's unabashed capitalism. Nevertheless, his father"s entrepreneurial flair did usefully endow young Morris with over £740 a year when he came of age, which gave him the freedom to choose his own career.

As a schoolboy at Marlborough, Morris spent his free time wandering across the chalk downland of Wiltshire, discovering its mysterious ancient stone circles and taking long walks through Savernake Forest. Schooldays were sufficiently un-demanding to allow him to spend hours absorbing both the visual and the historic charms of the surrounding district. Morris's unusually acute visual memory retained every nuance of form and colour. And it was these detailed images of English history and landscape that were the fount of his creative genius as a poet, painter, fabric designer and inspiration to the Arts and Crafts movement whose vision

VIEW OF THE CHAPEL, DORMITORY, AND OTHER BUILDINGS,
MARLBOROUGH COLLEGE, WILTS.

transformed the English house and garden. His profound and sensuous reponse to the English countryside was a constant thread in his writing and, most of all, it wove through his exuberant and rhythmical floral patterns, the finest of the Victorian age and unsurpassed today. From his devotion to the land he developed a love of birds, trees, water plants and luxuriant clusters of old-fashioned flowers.

Nicknamed 'Crab' at Marlborough, Morris is said to have regaled his companions during their walks and in the dormitory at night with an endless flow of fanciful tales of medieval knights – indeed some of them thought he was 'Welsh and mad'. Fellow pupils noted the characteristic restlessness of his fingers, energy which he channelled into making fishing nets, one end attached to a desk. By his last term, Morris was renowned for his knowledge of silkworms and old churches rather than for his scholarship. More positively, his love of architecture and ecclesiastical buildings had been fanned by the religious atmosphere of the school and he became a devout High Church Anglican, ready to study theology.

In 1848, Morris's widowed mother moved to Water House in Walthamstow, a smaller Georgian house only a few miles from Woodford Hall, and Morris returned to live there in 1851, following a pupils' rebellion at Marlborough which left the school in turmoil. He spent a year studying classics with a private tutor and resumed his daily walks and rides through Epping Forest. Once again, he was able to enjoy the quiet pleasures of a garden. In an obviously autobiographical story, written when he was in his thirties, but never published, he described what must have been a summer evening at Water House. As the hero takes a fork from the garden shed to work on the melon ground, Morris writes:

. . . for some strange reason that moment and the half hour were one of the unforgotten times of his life, and in after days he could never smell the mixed scent of a toolhouse, with its bast mats and earthy roots and herbs, in a hot summer evening, without that evening with every word spoken or gesture made coming up clear into his memory.

FAR LEFT Elm House, Clay Street, Walthamstow, now demolished, where Morris was born on 24 March 1834. It was then surrounded by the flattish, wooded plains of the Lea Valley.

LEFT Marlborough College, where Morris was enrolled in 1848. He spent his spare time rambling through Savernake Forest and over the Wiltshire Downs: 'very beautiful country,' he wrote, 'thickly scattered over with historical monuments'.

ABOVE RIGHT The Water House, Walthamstow, now the William Morris Gallery. On a landing window seat, the young William would sit reading, often for an entire day at a time.

BELOW RIGHT The extensive grounds of the Water House, now Lloyd Park, included a wide moat where Morris and his brothers and sisters went boating in summer and ice-skating in winter. They would also row to an island, covered in tangled growth, where Rendall, one of the brothers, marooned himself after reading Robinson Crusoe – but he returned to the house when it began to get dark.

29

DREAMING SPIRES

Morris proved to be an able scholar and won a place at Exeter College, Oxford. Almost from the first day, his constant friend was a young man of Welsh ancestry, Edward Burne-Jones, who was to become Morris's lifelong friend and artistic collaborator, and eventually a knight. At that time this pale, gangly son of a struggling picture framer was plain Ted Jones from Birmingham. Burne-Jones later described how Morris, a slim figure with hazel eyes and expressive mouth, had come 'tumbling in' on the first evening of a term and 'talked incessantly for seven hours or longer'. Morris, he said, was 'different from all the men I had ever met. He talked with vehemence and sometimes with violence. I never knew him languid or tired.'

The two undergraduates arrived in Oxford in 1853, soon after the university was opened to new sections of the community. Old restrictions had been removed and religious tests abolished. The population of Oxford had grown from 12,000 at the turn of the century to 28,000 and the city was bursting at the seams. Morris had to settle for temporary accommodation in a little quadrangle called Hell Quad, which looked directly on to the small, enclosed Fellows' Garden, with a side view of the lane leading to the Bodleian Library. Later, Morris and Burne-Jones lived in adjoining sets of rooms in the Prideaux Buildings on Broad Street. Neither liked Exeter much and they preferred to spend their time at Pembroke College with Burne-Jones's contemporaries from King Edward's School in Birmingham. Burne-Jones and Morris took fencing lessons and spent long afternoons in New College cloisters or Merton Chapel, and they sang Gregorian chants in the daily morning services at St Thomas's church.

LEFT Exeter College, where Morris studied, 1853–5. Oxford was 'an abiding influence and pleasure', and he was seized by the euphoria of living among Matthew Arnold's 'dreaming spires' and the 'last enchantments of the Middle Age'. With Edward Burne-Jones, he steeped himself in all aspects of medieval life.

RIGHT Duke Humphrey's Library at the Bodleian, where Morris spent hours studying and sketching from French and English medieval illuminated manuscripts.

Both young men were intent on becoming High Church clergymen, indeed they even considered founding a new type of monastery. However, the Anglo-Catholic fervour they had expected to find in Oxford was in decline. Ruskin and a passion for the Middle Ages filled the gap. After the publication of his *Modern Painters* (1843) and *Seven Lamps of Architecture* (1848), John Ruskin was hailed as the critic of the day, almost a prophet. He championed art, architecture, the Middle Ages, nature – and the Pre-Raphaelite painters, a controversial new group based in London. After falling under the spell of the writings of the influential artist and moralist, Morris and Burne-Jones began strolling through Oxford wearing purple trousers, convinced they must dedicate their lives to art.

ARTISTS AND INSPIRATION

Burne-Jones and Morris were excited by the work of the Pre-Raphaelite Brotherhood, founded in 1848 by John Everett Millais, William Holman Hunt, James Collinson, William Rossetti, Thomas Woolner, Frederick Stephens and, most importantly, Dante Gabriel Rossetti, who was to play such a bittersweet role in Morris's life. The group reacted against the grand and gloomy style of the old masters and determined instead to portray scenery, people and flowers naturally, in a manner faithful to life. 'Truth to Nature' was a principle adopted from their mentor Ruskin. Morris and Burne-Jones were able to study some of their finest work because Thomas Combe, the wealthy Oxford University printer, owned 21 Pre-Raphaelite paintings. They admired those by Rossetti most of all. His painting entitled *The First Anniversary of the Death of Beatrice* had a profound effect on the two undergraduates. Burne-Jones wrote that Rossetti's work filled them with the 'greatest wonder and delight . . . at once he seemed to us the chief figure in the Pre-Raphaelite Brotherhood'. Combe's wife helped the artists to work outside the studio, lending them props for their paintings and even packing hampers to take into the surrounding countryside in search of 'truth to nature' backgrounds. Burne-Jones made painstaking studies of foliage. Morris loved the flowers in Christ Church meadow, images of which – greater celandine, field maple, buttercup, ivy, oak, hogweed, whitethorn, briony – had been carved by a medieval mason on the St Frideswide's shrine in Christ Church cathedral. From Ruskin-inspired reverence for architecture was born admiration for both the flowers of the past and respect for formal structure.

FAR LEFT John Ruskin in his study at Brantwood, his Lake District home, 1882. 'Happiness is increased,' he wrote in his guidebook to the area, 'not by the enlargement of the possessions, but of the heart. If thus taught we had the making of our house and estate in our own hands, no manner of temperance in pleasure would be better rewarded than that of making our gardens gay only with common flowers.'

ABOVE The First Anniversary of the Death of Beatrice (1853–4), one of the watercolours by Dante Gabriel Rossetti that inspired Morris and Burne-Jones to devote themselves to art.

LEFT Dante Gabriel Rossetti, the magnetic leader of the Pre-Raphaelite Brotherhood, photographed by Charles Dodgson (better known as Lewis Carroll) in 1883.

With their passion for the Middle Ages, Morris and Burne-Jones were deeply affected by being in what was still then mostly a medieval city. It was famously described by Matthew Arnold, whose poem 'The Scholar Gypsy' appeared in 1853 and enthralled romantic Oxford. Oxford was, as Morris said, 'an abiding influence and pleasure in my life', and it contributed to his early ideas of what a garden should look like. From college days came the fascination with enclosed medieval monastery gardens. Although the arbours of clipped shrubs, trellises smothered by rampant climbers, fruit trees, formal beds of medicinal and culinary herbs and flowers had long gone, the structure was much the same as when the gardens were tended by medieval gardeners.

Living amid the Gothic architecture of Oxford, studying medieval works in the Bodleian Library and reading Malory's tales of King Arthur all added to Morris's preoccupation with the romantic past. Ruskin had revived interest in illuminated medieval manuscripts in which references to gardens of delight were common.

Morris also devoured Chaucer's descriptions of gardens. In *Troilus and Criseyde* garden beds are divided by wands or railings and sanded paths; in his translation of the *Roman de la Rose*, gardens are enclosed 'by mesuring, right even and square in compassing'. The poor widow of *The Nun's Priest's Tale* grew centaury, fumitory, caper spurge, hellebore, spurge laurel and ground ivy.

Before leaving Oxford, Morris used part of his inheritance to launch the *Oxford and Cambridge Magazine* and its first issue, in January 1856, contained his essay about a medieval stone mason, 'The Story of the Unknown Church'. It is important because it was Morris's first detailed description of a garden to be published. The story paints a vivid picture of an ancient, round-arched, church cloister surrounding a lawn, with a marble fountain in the centre and massed sunflowers at the edge. Further on there is a less formal area encircled by poplar trees that contains tall spires of hollyhocks, convolvulus, nasturtiums and more trellises covered with roses. Wild flowers, Morris wrote, had 'crept into the garden from without: lush green briony and the red berry and purple, yellow-spiked flower of deadly nightshade, all growing together in the glorious days of early autumn'.

Gardens of delight where lords and ladies danced, sang, made music and dallied with 'courtly love' were common in late medieval manuscripts and they fascinated Morris, Rossetti and Burne-Jones. This scene, called 'Carolle in the Garden', from a late fifteenth-century copy of the Roman de la Rose *by Guillaume de la Lorris, is one of many illustrations that influenced Morris's theories on gardening.*

At the age of 22, Morris had already evolved the formula for his future gardens: a formal framework paying tribute to tradition and based on the medieval *hortus conclusus*, a small enclosed garden; naturalistic planting to soften the straight lines of paths and hedges; and some native flowers in deference to the local countryside.

His theories on gardens were forming at a time when gardening as a pastime was no longer the preserve of owners of grand houses. It was becoming a consuming interest among the middle classes who settled in the new suburbs that spread like a rash across the country. Tens of thousands of new gardens were being created each year, but Morris detested the sterility of these suburban plots, especially those laid out like miniature parks. He developed an aversion to the hard-looking, Italianate gardens which sprouted in the Home Counties.

TOWARDS A TRUE VOCATION

Morris believed the highest form of art was architecture. During two vacations he toured the glorious ancient churches and cathedrals of northern France and the Low Countries – experiences that powerfully affected him, and affirmed his taste for northern Gothic. He decided that architecture rather than holy orders should be his career.

After graduating in 1856, he went to study architecture in Oxford, under the Gothic Revivalist George Edmund Street, but he found the discipline of daily work at an architect's desk restricting. Within the year, he was in London, persuaded to take up painting by the urbane and glamorous artist Dante Gabriel Rossetti, a leader of the original Pre-Raphaelite Brotherhood. Burne-Jones was already learning painting as a pupil of Rossetti, having left Oxford without taking his degree.

In London, Morris and Burne-Jones revelled in the company of Rossetti and his friends, and between them they gave new impetus to the flagging Pre-Raphaelite movement. Through Rossetti they met John Ruskin and the poets Robert Browning and his wife Elizabeth Barrett Browning. Morris and Burne-Jones moved into rooms at Upper Gordon Street in Bloomsbury, which they decorated with brasses of ancient knights and drawings by Albrecht Dürer. When the two men moved again, it was to Rossetti's old rooms at 17 Red Lion Square in Bloomsbury, where Morris commissioned the first furniture made to his own design – rather hefty, painted pieces in medieval style. He had yet to find his vocation. He turned his hand to one craft after another, learning to model in clay, to carve in wood and stone, and to illuminate manuscripts to a standard that impressed Ruskin; he even tried embroidery. But the perfect outlet for his creative energy was still to come.

LOVE AND MARRIAGE

Some of the early Pre-Raphaelites met the group's newer members in 1857 for the painting of the Oxford Union Debating Hall. Millais, Rossetti and Holman Hunt joined Morris, Burne-Jones, Arthur Hughes and Alexander Munro – with Ruskin and Algernon Swinburne looking on. They had been commissioned to paint the ten bays of the upper walls and to pattern the open-timbered roof. Morris persuaded the group to illustrate the Arthurian legends for which he still had a passion. Known affectionately as 'Top' or 'Topsy' because of his unruly mass of hair, Morris, in his youthful enthusiasm, wore chain mail. The walls of the Union looked, it is said, like the margin of an illuminated manuscript, but alas, Galahad and Guenevere soon faded because the artists failed to prepare the surfaces properly. Of the romantic Pre-Raphaelite imagery, only Alexander Munro's sculptural effects over the door remain. Years later Morris re-painted part of the chamber, but it has since faded again.

The Oxford Union venture was to change Morris's life. On a visit to a local theatre, Rossetti spotted what he called 'a stunner' in the audience. She was seventeen-year-old Jane Burden, dark-haired, full-lipped, and with strikingly angular features, the daughter of a stablehand. With her parents' permission, she agreed to sit as an artist's model for Rossetti and later for Morris. Morris was smitten. He knew he had to compete with the more magnetic and sophisticated Rossetti to win her favour, but he lacked experience in wooing women, often finding himself tongue-tied and handicapped by an unfortunately gruff manner.

The stress of courtship, increased by savage criticism of his recently published poetry, 'The Defence of Guenevere' (short lyrical verses combining the Arthurian legends with love poems to Jane), led to a bout of ill health after his engagement to Jane was announced in 1858. Morris idolized Jane as a romantic, almost medieval figure, but in reality theirs was an unlikely match between a rumbustious, somewhat self-centred middle-class

maverick and a frail and withdrawn working-class beauty in need of financial security. None of his family attended the wedding in Oxford in 1859. Neither did Rossetti. As a wedding present, Burne-Jones painted scenes from Chaucer's *Prioress's Tale* on a wardrobe cabinet for them. Jane was the model for the Virgin. On the inside of the doors, Morris began, but never finished, six figures with his bride as *Queen Guenevere Disrobing in a Medieval Chamber*. The couple set off on a six-week honeymoon, touring Morris's favourite parts of Europe – Bruges, northern France and the Rhine. And Morris embarked upon what was probably the happiest five years of his life.

The partnership is often represented as an uneven one, but Jane made an enormous contribution to Morris's artistic range. She became an expert needlewoman in her own right, working on his hangings and appliqué. Jane wrote: 'We studied old pieces by unpicking them. We learnt very much but it was uphill work and only carried through by his enormous energy and perseverance.'

In those early days of marriage, Morris's talents began to lead him towards the decorative arts. Through these, and through his writing, he at last found his ideal means of creative expression combining art, history and nature. In the three decades that followed he produced the most extraordinarily wide-ranging body of work: seven volumes of poetry; ten books of prose, including prose and verse translation; two volumes of lectures; over 500 repeating designs for wallpaper, textiles, embroidery, carpets and tapestry; hundreds of individual designs for textiles and stained glass; 52 book titles in 66 volumes with 650 different designs and borders to ornament the pages from his own press; and a style of house and garden that was to become classic.

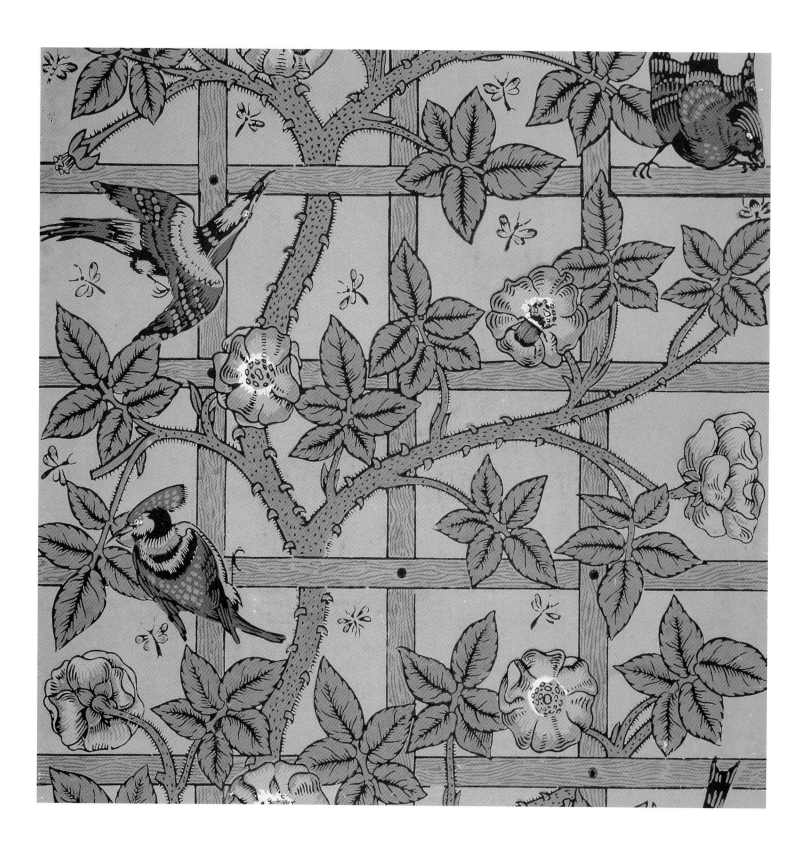

THE RED HOUSE

ORRIS WAS TRAVELLING IN FRANCE with Philip Webb, an architect who had become his friend while he was working in Street's office, when he made initial jottings of plans for the Red House on a copy of Murray's *Guide to France*. The two-acre site chosen by Morris was an old, abandoned orchard with an adjoining meadow in fertile, gently rolling countryside near the village of Upton, at Bexleyheath in Kent. The nearby valleys of the Cray and the Darenth satisfied Morris's need to live near a river. To provide historical resonance, the remains of an Augustinian priory and ancient Watling Street – the route taken by Chaucer's Canterbury pilgrims – were close by. Rossetti was delighted to discover that the nearest hamlet was known as Hog's Hole.

From the start, the garden was designed as an integral part of the Red House and details of the trees and climbing plants appear on the original drawings. Webb listed 80 trees on the site, many of them old and twisted fruit trees including apple, cherry, pear, plum, damson and quince, as well as oak, ash, yew, hazel and holly. Morris was determined that there would be minimal disturbance to mature trees, preserving as many of them as possible so that the L-shaped red brick house would appear to sit naturally in the orchard. When it was finished, so close were some trees to the house that, it is said, ripe apples would occasionally bounce through the open windows on warm autumn evenings.

Building began in 1859 and there were still some workmen on the site when Morris and his new wife arrived in the summer of 1860. Built of brick and oak, with a steeply pitched, irregular

ABOVE Morris in his smock (c. 1876).

LEFT Trellis, 1884, Morris's first wallpaper design, with birds drawn by Philip Webb.

tiled roof, windows of every shape and size, deep porches and Gothic arches, the visionary Red House was, according to Morris, 'very medieval in spirit'.

Morris's profound respect for pre-Renaissance England and for the integrity of the countryside combined to create something new when he built the Red House. By using local workmen and work methods and traditional local building materials, and by revealing rather than hiding the construction, he made the Red House, according to Nikolaus Pevsner in *Pioneers of the Modern Movement* (1936), the precursor of the Modern movement in architecture. The building was revolutionary both for its emphasis on the vernacular and because the outside appearance was an expression of the interior requirements.

The garden was as idiosyncratic as the house, reflecting Morris's and Webb's talent for drawing on the past to create something surprisingly innovative. In contrast to the asymmetric building, the garden was symmetrical, following Ruskin's theory that straight lines suggested restraint and provided contrast with the natural curves of the plants. With Webb, who was equally committed to an integrated house and garden, Morris created the prototype for the Arts and Crafts garden a generation before Gertrude Jekyll established the style in her writing and designs (see page 87). Webb was a keen naturalist, interested in plants and animals, especially birds, and, like Morris, had a taste for 'old-fashioned' gardens. The Morris/Webb ideas were not historical revivalism but strove to devise new forms embracing nature and tradition.

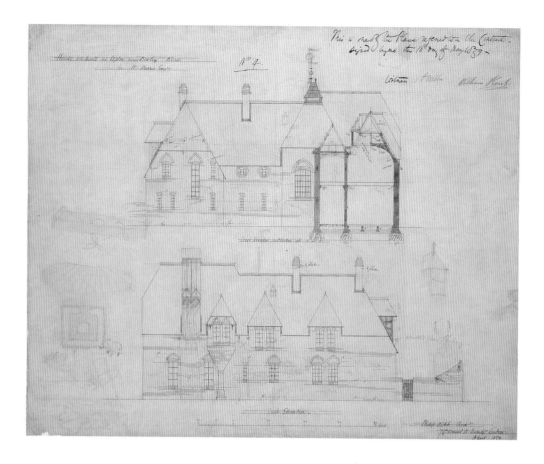

LEFT Designed with his friend Philip Webb, Morris's Red House was a milestone in suburban architecture. Webb's plan for the west and east elevations shows some of the original features that made it a key building of the Arts and Crafts movement, and one of the most influential small houses of the nineteenth century. The German scholar Hermann Multhesius described it as the 'first private house of the new artistic culture, the first house to be conceived as a whole inside and out, the very first example in the history of the modern house'. A sketch for the square front garden appears on the far left of the plan.

RIGHT The well-house courtyard garden photographed by Emery Walker, c. 1900. The garden was conceived as an integral part of the design – jasmine and other climbers that clothed its walls were listed on the plans.

The Red House gave Morris the opportunity to create an outdoor setting that broke the mould of stiff Victorian gardens. The plans show his determination to ensure that the outer surroundings were in harmony with the house. White jasmine, honeysuckle and rose clambered up the red brick walls, forging a floral link with the grounds.

Georgiana, wife of Burne-Jones, described in a letter the flowering creepers, which were planted against the walls from the earliest possible time, 'so there was no look of raw newness about it'. The garden, she said, 'beautified beforehand by the apple trees', quickly took shape. Georgiana, Morris's wife Jane – affectionately called Janey – and other women friends did their needlework in the drawing room overlooking the bowling alley. Views from the house led through different aspects of the garden to the countryside beyond. Morris's daughter May later described the garden:

. . . so happily English in its sweetness and freshness, with its rose hedges and lavender and rosemary borders to the flowerbeds, its alley and bowling green and the orchard walks among the apple trees.

May, although only three years old when the Morris family left the Red House, remembered being with her sister and throwing rose petals on to the face of the poet Algernon Swinburne while he was lying in the long grass in the orchard.

Morris decreed that 'a garden should be divided and made to look like so many flower-closes in a meadow, or a wood'. Accordingly, the front garden was square, with a path leading straight to the front door, and a hedge provided shelter from the wind. The inner garden was divided into four, small, interconnecting squares defined by wattle, their formality softened with thickly trained roses to make natural flowery arbours, each

like an external 'room' with its own distinct decoration. Throughout the garden Morris used the wattle fences and hedges – as well as trees, avenues and grass walks – as boundaries for the 'rooms'.

A separate area was created in the L-shape of the house, the walls forming two sides of a semi-courtyard and the two open sides enclosed by more rose-entwined wattle. In the centre was one of the most striking features, a well-house with a circular brick surround and massive oak posts. Its tall, conical, tiled roof was both Gothic and reminiscent of the Kentish oast houses.

The simple words of verse that Morris penned and Jane embroidered on a bed coverlet convey the beauty of the Red House garden:

> I know a little garden-close
> Set thick with lily and red rose,
> Where I would wander if I might
> From dewy morn to dewy night,
> And have one with me wandering.

The house proved to be a catalyst in changing the direction of Morris's career. It was the cradle of a craft co-operative which, in 1861, became Morris, Marshall, Faulkner and Company with its first workshops and offices at Red Lion Square. Having difficulty in buying the right furnishings for the Red House, Morris and Webb began designing and making their own, helped by Burne-Jones, Rossetti and other members of their circle. Calling themselves 'fine art workmen', they went on to become commercial manufacturers of furniture, stained glass, painted tiles and embroidery. Fabrics and wallpapers followed. Among early orders were 'works illustrative of the legends and romances of the Middle Ages'. The Firm, as it was known, was praised for

its display of stained glass and furniture in the Medieval Court at the 1862 International Exhibition in South Kensington.

AN EARTHLY PARADISE

While many fellow Victorians needed great mountains and sweeping deserts to stir their senses, Morris celebrated the charm and understated beauty of the Essex marshland and the wooded hills of Kent. In the same way, he delighted in growing simple local flowers, giving them equal ranking in the garden with imported plants, setting them alongside one another as he did in his patterns. He liked a 'natural combination' of flowers and shunned the contemporary showy blooms which Ruskin condemned in typically thundering, Old Testament terms as 'pampered and bloated above their natural size, stewed and heated into diseased growth, corrupted by evil communication into speckled and inharmonious colours'.

Morris was certainly responsible for much of the garden. In later years his biographer, John Mackail, was struck by the imaginative design, and Morris, he said, had good reason to pride himself on his knowledge of gardening:

ABOVE In Morris's unfinished painting on the cupboard in the hall of the Red House his idea of paradise includes his own orchard and his friends as models. Based on Malory's Morte d'Arthur, *in which Sir Lancelot brings Sir Tristram to the castle of Joyous Gard, here Burne-Jones offers fruit to a woman seated on the ground while Rossetti's fiancée Lizzie Siddal is leaning against a tree.*

RIGHT Built within an orchard, the Red House is enclosed by trees which are heavy with blossom in spring. Even today, house and garden represent an idyllic retreat from the world.

LEFT *Captured in the internal angle of the L-shaped Red House, the well-house stands as centrepiece. One of the most idiosyncratic and charming features of the garden, it has a tall conical roof and oak supports, its red brick matching that of the main house. The well-house was originally enclosed by a rose-covered trellis.*

ABOVE *Panels of glass featuring flower motifs decorate the windows.*

RIGHT *The windows of the Red House are the key to its original design. They appear in various shapes and sizes, according to the demands of the interior. Views of the garden from every angle and natural light give the house and its setting a special harmony.*

. . . of flowers and vegetable and fruit trees he knew all the ways and capabilities. Red House garden, with its long walks, its mid-summer lilies and autumn sunflowers, its wattle rose-trellises enclosing richly-flowered square garden plots, was then as unique as the house it surrounded.

During his years at the Red House, Morris embarked on the epic that was to make his name as a poet, *The Earthly Paradise*, a narrative poem written in Chaucerian metre, consisting of a prologue and 24 tales which relate legends in the Greek and Norse tradition. In an episode from the 'Quest of Jason', the garden of Circe resembles that of the Red House:

> A lovely pleasance, set with flowers, foursquare,
> On three sides ending in a cloister fair
> That hid the fair feet of a marble house,
> Carved thick with flowers and stories amorous,
> And midmost of the slender garden trees . . .

Curiously, Morris's talents as a poet have been largely forgotten today, yet he was famous for his verse and was considered for the post of poet laureate after Tennyson died, a flattering proposal which he declined, being unable to imagine himself composing official odes. He continued to write not only poetry but letters, journalism and lectures throughout all his other endeavours.

From the Red House garden, Morris and his friends enjoyed views over the Kent countryside, through which they made expeditions in Morris's decorated cart. Locals must have gaped at the vehicle, clattering past with its unconventional cargo of arty-looking young gentlemen and their uncorseted ladies, brightly dressed in flowing, medieval-inspired garments. One observer remarked acidly that they looked like 'the advance guard of a travelling show'.

Flowers and foliage from the garden found their way into the new Pre-Raphaelite paintings, Burne-Jones once rising before dawn to make a study of a poppy. Morris made sketches of lilies, sunflowers and other plants, which were subsequently reproduced in his wallpaper and textiles. In 1862, Morris produced his first three commercial designs for wallpapers: *Daisy*, *Fruit* and *Trellis*. They were inspired by the trailing roses, fruit trees and flowers in the new garden. *Trellis*, with its climbing

THE EARTHLY PARADISE.

A caricature of Morris in search of the earthly paradise 'where none grow old'.

roses and birds, reveals Morris's fascination with medieval gardens – similar images of flower-covered trellises appear in many medieval paintings. Morris particularly liked the contrast of the simple motif of sinuous stems against a background of squares.

Family life flourished at the Red House. Morris encouraged his wife's talent for needlework and, with the birth in 1861 and 1862 of their two daughters, Jenny and May, he discovered the pleasures of fatherhood. Jane's spinster sister, Bessie Burden, came to live with them after their father died and she, too, emerged as a consummate needlewoman, later becoming a technical instructor at the Royal School of Needlework. At weekends, friends such as Edward and Georgiana Burne-Jones,

46

The Summons, tapestry, designed in 1890, from the Holy Grail *series, one of the last Morris worked on. Thirty years after he designed his first fabric designs, he used similar patterns of simple flowers – and managed to include three birds.*

Rossetti and his wife Lizzie Siddal, and Ford Madox Brown would arrive for joyous house parties, contributing to house decorations, playing bowls and parlour games, spending evenings singing songs at the piano and eating hearty suppers. Morris, who had developed a love of food and wine while on his travels in France, would plunge down to the cellar and emerge, beaming, with armfuls of bottles.

In 1865, after five fulfilling years at the Red House, Morris suffered a severe bout of rheumatic fever, and the strain of travelling ten miles into London every day, combined with a drop in income after the Firm had taken a lease on large premises at 26 Queen Square in Bloomsbury, forced the family to move back to live in town. Morris abandoned his dream of establishing a colony of artists and craftsmen at the Red House. He, his wife, two daughters, Bessie, the nanny and other household servants

settled in spacious rooms 'above the shop' in Queen Square. Morris could never bear to go back to the Red House and eventually he sold it. Georgiana Burne-Jones said that for years afterwards the house would appear, like a childhood home, in the dreams of their friends.

A GROWING FIRM

Despite chaotic finances, the Firm prospered, being awarded important public commissions to decorate rooms at St James's Palace and the South Kensington Museum (now the Victoria & Albert). George Warington Taylor, who was briefly business manager of the Firm, battled against Morris's tendency to take on too much work and not finish it, as well as his extravagance and a propensity to spend profits on wine and books: 'You must reduce your wine consumption to two and a half bottles a day . . . this will save somewhere about £68 a year,' he wrote sternly. He succeeded in injecting some discipline into the company.

The Queen Square workshops were enlarged to deal with a growing order book and for seven years Morris lived and worked in the same dwelling in the manner of the medieval craftsmen he so admired. May recalled the large easel in her father's studio, and the bread he used for erasing, 'a huge lump of bread with a small hole picked out of the middle stationed on a chair or anywhere handy, and the floor bestrewn with breadcrumbs'. Morris's greatest pleasure in life was his work. The Firm was going from strength to strength, with the partners, including Webb, Rossetti and Madox Brown, supervising an extraordinary output of tapestries, wall-paintings, wallpapers, stained glass, sculpture, tiles, furniture, metalwork, jewellery and embroidery. Many early commissions were for church windows, others were for private houses.

Unusually for a man of his means in those days, Morris donned a workman's smock and mastered many of the crafts, taking pride in being as close as possible to his ideal, the artist-craftsman. Such was Morris's versatility that he became skilled at any art which took his fancy, plunging into the intricacies of each one with obsessive intensity. His creative power derived not only from his fertile imagination, but also from his virtuoso manual talents, a thoroughgoing knowledge of technical processes and an intuitive flair for handling materials. He became so expert at medieval illumination and calligraphy that Rossetti claimed he was unrivalled by any contemporary. He rose early each morning to weave exquisite tapestries on his handloom and write poetry.

But it was in pattern design that he proved to be without equal and here he found expression for his deep feelings for history and nature. He spent months in the industrial town of Leek, Staffordshire, at Thomas Wardle's dye works, experimenting with natural vegetable dyes and reviving the neglected art of organic colouring of textiles. The lessons of history were always with him:

However original a man may be he cannot afford to disregard the works of art that have been produced in times past . . . he is bound to study old examples, but he is also bound to supplement that by a careful study of nature.

Jasmine Trellis, *Morris's first printed fabric pattern, was designed at the end of the 1860s and block printed on cotton. Although drawn several years after his first wallpaper,* Trellis, *it still has a similar design, using the strong cross-hatching of trellis work.*

He insisted on an impression of flow and movement within a precise and orderly structure. 'Ornamental pattern-work,' he said, 'must possess three qualities: beauty, imagination and order . . . order invents certain beautiful and natural forms, which will remind not only of nature but also of much that lies beyond.' As for embroidery, he instructed his workers to remember, 'We are gardening with silk and gold thread.'

At Queen Square, apart from a paved yard and the communal central gardens with their London plane trees and gloomy evergreens, there was no garden for May and Jenny. May buried her doll in one of the flowerboxes near the stained-glass painters' workroom and was banned from playing there.

In 1867, Jane resumed her role as an artist's model for Rossetti, who was by then a widower. His wife, the highly strung artist Lizzie Siddal, had suffered a mental breakdown after her daughter was stillborn in the same year that Morris's elder daughter, Jenny, was born. Nine months later she died of an overdose of laudanum. Jane herself endured ill health of a mysterious, unspecified nature which appeared to worsen in the shadow of Rossetti's obsessive attentions. She suffered an elegant collapse in 1869 and the ever-solicitous Morris took her to a German spa for two months, but the following year she was still ailing. Even so, Jane risked scandal by spending a month with Rossetti at a cottage in Scalands in Sussex in 1870. They certainly became lovers during this time together, which appears to have precipitated the need for a permanent retreat in the country where they could discreetly conduct their affair. Despite the liaison, Rossetti was still Morris's business partner and remained a friend.

49

KELMSCOTT MANOR

IN 1871, AFTER TWELVE YEARS OF MARRIAGE – six years of which had been spent in Queen Square – Morris saw an advertisement for a house to let in Oxfordshire and went with Rossetti to look at it. For £75 per annum, they immediately took joint tenancy of the house and its 68 acres, divided into 'closes' or small fields. Kelmscott Manor, near Lechlade, in the manor of Broadwell, Oxfordshire, lay between the village and the 'stripling Thames'. It was the only truly rural house and garden in which Morris ever lived. Morris wrote to Charles Faulkner, a partner in the Firm:

> I have been looking about for a house for the wife and kids . . . a heaven on earth; an old stone Elizabethan house like Water Eaton, and such a garden! Close down on the river, a boat house and all things handy.

Although he stayed there only for short periods, Kelmscott was an important influence on Morris's Arts and Crafts philosophy. The building, a gabled, three-storeyed sixteenth- and seventeenth-century manor house, was built of the local grey-coloured limestone, with a stone-slate roof and mullioned windows. It was surrounded by tall elms and stone barns, and the extensive grounds ran down to water meadows, with the narrow river flowing beyond.

Kelmscott is a prime example of English – specifically Oxfordshire – vernacular architecture, based on the ready availability of Cotswold stone. It was Morris who gave it the courtesy title of 'manor'. He had no manorial rights, but he was treated as the squire. Although the East Gloucestershire Railway had just opened, when he first took the tenancy there was no station closer than Faringdon, seven miles away, until in 1873 a station was built north of Lechlade, only three miles away, making the house accessible as a weekend retreat. But winter damp and flooding meant that it became more a part-time summer residence. Rossetti's brother, William, described the isolated situation of Kelmscott in his diary: 'When the weather breaks the whole country is under water; and he [Rossetti] used of late to be going in a boat over the meadows whereon he had previously been walking.'

For Jane, visiting Kelmscott was a return to her roots. She had lost contact with her parents after her marriage and had not attended her mother's funeral in Oxford earlier in 1871. Her mother came from Alvescot, only a few miles away across the fields, and to the south-east lay her father's birthplace at Stanton Harcourt.

Morris revelled in the unchanged rhythms of life in an ancient house, where there were also still traces of the original garden. Many of his descriptions in *News from Nowhere* convey this sense of belonging and the continuity of rural existence. The gabled manor was, in many ways, the antithesis of the Red House: old rather than new; stone instead of brick; a random series of rooms on different levels rather than a spacious, orderly interior. There were spectacular projecting rainwater chutes and a triple-seater privy at the end of the garden instead of an inside WC – the manor had neither running water nor electricity.

As for the garden at Kelmscott, it was established and laid out in a traditional manner, unlike the garden at the Red House, which was an orchard turned into a garden. The soil was

ABOVE *Morris in 1873, photographed at the Burne-Joneses' home, The Grange, in London.*

LEFT Kennet, *1883, a design first printed on silk, named after a tributary of the Thames.*

ABOVE This photograph of Kelmscott Manor from the gate, taken in the 1930s, shows the walled garden in front of the original sixteenth-century house and the 1670 additions to the right.

LEFT Today a profusion of climbing plants still scrambles over the porch at Kelmscott Manor, through which thousands of tourists enter each summer.

The large, gabled house, built of local Thames Valley stone, is now owned by the Society of Antiquaries. It was the home to which Morris was most attached. He loved its quirky rooms and passageways, the nearby cluster of farm buildings and the grounds skirting the infant river, where he fished in the afternoons. There are no plant lists from the time when Morris lived at Kelmscott, although his letters give detailed descriptions of some of the flowers and trees.

light and alluvial compared to the Kentish clay. To Morris's gratification, the garden more than halfway approached his ideal, with straight paths and separate 'rooms' bounded by old yew hedges. Even Rossetti, writing to his mother in 1871, said, 'The garden is a perfect paradise.' Borrowing a phrase from Tennyson, whose poetry he had illustrated fifteen years earlier, Rossetti called Kelmscott 'A haunt of ancient peace'. He, like Morris, delighted in its unchanging rhythms:

> A most lovely house . . . It still belongs to the family whose ancestors built it, and whose arms are still on some of the chimney breasts. The garden, and meadows leading to the river bank, are truly delicious – indeed the place is perfect; and the riverside walks are most charming in their way, though I must say the flatness of the country renders it monotonous and uninspiring to me.

In his letters, Rossetti described the snowdrops in the garden and 'fat cut hedges that seemed to purr and simmer in the sun'. Morris made regular attacks with shears on the yew hedge under the gable of the tapestry room, giving a vigorous clipping to the topiary dragon, which he named Fafnir, after the dragon in his Icelandic saga, *The Story of Sigurd the Volsung* (1876). Another equally dramatic yew hedge had an arched opening.

In his biography of Rossetti, Evelyn Waugh described with affection the little door in the stone wall, which opens into the walled garden at Kelmscott, and the modest porch. Both door and porch were alterations by Philip Webb. (A photograph of Jane and her daughters in the early 1900s shows dog-roses entwined in its white wooden trellis.) Waugh continues:

> There is no drive up to the house . . . a narrow strip of paved path between clipped yews – one of them a very fine dragon, designed by Morris himself . . . There must have been a good deal of bumping of heads. The rooms, which lead from each other, are low and small, darkened with paint and patterned hangings; there are little embrasures filled with china, in which there is just room to stand alone. The garden, too, is tiny and ornamental, set out in little paths where two cannot walk abreast, bordered by low box hedges, and walled with mellow Cotswold stone and great ramparts of yew.

The decorated capital from The Story of Sigurd the Volsung *shows the dragon, Fafnir. The dragon leaped from the pages of the Icelandic saga into his garden, demonstrating the cross-fertilization between Morris's gardens, books and design.*

Rural Kelmscott had changed little over the centuries and the manor grounds contained the time-honoured blend of fruit trees and bushes, vegetable patches, including an asparagus bed, and borders filled with cottage flowers. Ash, elder, elm, poplar and willow grew within the walls, made from local oolitic limestone, while elm and willow stood on the outer side. A straight, flagstone path, punctuated on either side with standard roses, led through the formal front garden to the porch. On the west side of the house was a paved yard with elm trees filled with nesting rooks; on the east, a garden with shrubs and flower beds. Southwards, beyond a fine stone barn, a dovecote and a cluster of grey stone sheds, there were meadows of seeding grasses extending to river

ABOVE The dovecote atop a grey stone shed, reminiscent of News from Nowhere: *'the doves were cooing on the roof-ridge, the rooks in the high elm trees beyond . . . and the swifts wheeled shirring about the gables.'*

RIGHT Morris would vigorously clip his topiary dragon, named Fafnir after the dragon in his Icelandic saga.

banks where willow grew among swathes of purple loosestrife. From the manor, a lane ran between ancient hawthorn hedges, smothered in summer by scrambling wild roses, leading to the village and the old Plough Inn, and further to St George's Church.

Morris could hardly improve the scene. Even in indifferent weather he would carry out what he called 'garden strolling', making detailed notes of plants as they flowered and then faded. On a cold and windy day in April 1895, he wrote to his daughter, Jenny:

The snowdrops nearly but not quite gone, a few purple crocuses, but of course not open on this sunless day, the daphne very full of blossom . . . The beautiful hepatica, which I used to love so when I was quite a little boy, in full bloom, both pink and blue . . .

The significance of the garden was explained in 1984 by the garden historian Mavis Batey, in an essay on Gertrude Jekyll (in *Artist, Gardener, Craftswoman*, edited by Michael Tooley):

It was the Morris cult of the old manor house with its old-fashioned orderly pleasure garden which would inspire the Arts and Crafts movement. Kelmscott was much more redolent of the past than an imagined medieval garden. It seemed to

55

belong rightfully to the old Elizabethan house and was a fulfilment of the wider ideal of a home which had 'grown up out of the soil' and the lives of the people who had lived there.

She continues:

The flat, reedy river landscape was ideal for a dreamer and [his] writings are full of its green meadows, ripened seeding grasses, larks, warblers, cow parsley, swans, reeds, herons, vetch, wild roses, rooks and hawthorn. He loved the landscape, not just for its quiet beauty, but for the materials it produced that could be spun back into the old house. . . . he collected reeds, grasses, roots, flowers and willow twigs for making dyes and studied the plants and birds which were favourite designs for his textiles.

JANE AND ROSSETTI

Morris did not immediately find the contentment he longed for at Kelmscott Manor. A personal sorrow marred those early years: the relationship between his wife and Rossetti. Partly to escape this emotional turmoil, Morris made two long trips to Iceland in the early 1870s, setting off on the first journey soon after he had settled the family at Kelmscott, leaving Jane alone with Rossetti, the servants and the children. In his first letter from Iceland to his wife, he finished with the words, 'Good-bye my dear, I have so often thought of the sweet fresh garden at Kelmscott and you and the little ones in it, and wished you happy.'

Morris had travelled throughout Europe, but he developed a special fascination with Icelandic culture and literature. He particularly admired the sagas, heroic tales of Nordic derring-do from the tenth and eleventh centuries, which appealed to his taste for the Gothic. He immersed himself in the intricacies of the language, with Icelandic scholar Eiríkr Magnússon as a tutor. These expeditions through bleak and desolate landscapes gave Morris's poetry new vigour and power and inspired the four-volume epic, *The Story of Sigurd the Volsung*.

Meanwhile, Jane's brooding, beautiful face was immortalized in a succession of sensual, romantic portraits by Rossetti. He adored Jane and, although he painted a total of 57 studies of her,

the best were done at Kelmscott. Some of his most characteristic Pre-Raphaelite images were the result of long sittings in the studio on the first floor – *Aurea Catena*, *La Donna della Fiamma*, *Mariana*, *Pandora*, *The Prisoner's Daughter*, *Proserpine*, *The Rose-leaf* and *The Water-Willow*. Most of them were replete with the suppressed desire that smouldered in so many Pre-Raphaelite paintings. Glimpses of Kelmscott are in many of the backgrounds, either the meadows, the river, the distant Lechlade spire, or the local foliage. In *Proserpine*, English ivy, *Hedera helix*, representing 'clinging memory', is shown (see page 123), just as it climbed up the walls of the house.

Refusing to interpret the marriage bond as a property contract, Morris refrained from interfering in Jane and Rossetti's romance; indeed, he enabled them to spend time together. But while Morris appeared to accept his wife's attachment to the more worldly artist, his private anguish is evident in his verse. In a letter to a friend, he refers to Rossetti's presence at Kelmscott Manor as 'a kind of slur on it'. Apologizing for his 'pettiness' in mentioning the subject, he writes:

OPPOSITE and ABOVE Drawings and photographs of Kelmscott Manor. The drawings, by E. H. New, done for Mackail's life of Morris, 1899, and the photographs, taken in the 1930s, show areas of the garden from the north and the west. Dramatic walls of yew, wattle fences, low box hedges and a 'superabundance' of flowers in the borders, 'looking orderly and rich', illustrate Morris's principles of garden design.

Rossetti has set himself down at Kelmscott as if he never meant to go away; and not only does that keep me away from the harbour of refuge (because it really is a farce our meeting when we can help it) but also he has all sorts of ways so unsympathetic with the sweet, simple old place . . .

May Morris remembered from her childhood the wild games of hide-and-seek with Rossetti's bohemian visitors, and the artist's erratic behaviour, coming down late to breakfast at the manor and eating an extraordinary number of eggs. Evelyn Waugh described Rossetti's daily routine, which began:

ABOVE *Morris loved water and often used plants of marsh and stream as motifs in his designs, none more so than the willow growing beside the river at Kelmscott. In* News from Nowhere, *he wrote about 'the meadow by the riverside, where lay our boat . . . saw the bleak speckling the water under the willow boughs . . . heard the great chub splashing here and there . . . and felt almost back in my boyhood.'*

RIGHT *Rossetti painted* The Water-Willow *in 1871. Jane Morris is holding sprigs of willow from the water meadows, and the River Thames and the gabled roofs of Kelmscott Manor are seen in the background. At Kelmscott, she and Rossetti conducted a passionate affair away from the public gaze. He plainly adored her, and produced a succession of sensual, intensely romantic portraits.*

... somewhere about noon, and, except for occasional furtive stumpings along with the river-bank with George Hake, did not include much fresh air or any exercise. He dined at ten, when the Morrises were going to bed, and fell into his first drugged slumber at about three or four ... he was impatient with the limitations of country life, and any criticism was blasphemy to Morris.

Rossetti's late hours were parodied by his friend Lewis Carroll, the Oxford don, in his verse 'The Hunting of the Snark':

> Its habit of getting up late you'll agree
> That it carries too far, when I say
> That it frequently breakfasts at five-o'clock tea,
> And dines on the following day.

Wholesome surroundings did little to help Rossetti, who spent long periods alone at Kelmscott in between Jane's visits from London. He was showing signs of increasing mental instability, aggravated by overuse of the drug chloral, sometimes mixed with whisky, which he originally took for insomnia. Delusions and paranoia led to his quitting the manor, after shouting abuse at a group of local fishermen when he imagined they had made an insulting remark. Rossetti and Jane were together for the last time at Kelmscott in the final week of May 1874. In July, he left for good, but delayed packing his many belongings. He continued to see Jane for a further two years. Finally, she said, she distanced herself from him for the sake of her daughters. She had discovered the extent of his chloral addiction in the winter of 1875–6, while she and young May were staying at Rossetti's rented villa at Aldwick near Bognor, Sussex.

In his letters from Bognor, Rossetti referred to Morris as 'Morris the gardener' when inquiring about the garden in Kelmscott. In another, he wrote: 'I should be glad to hear that the man in the house, being a gardener, was doing something in the garden as he proposed, and should be willing to pay a cheap assistant which was his plan.'

Rossetti remained devoted to Jane until his death in 1882. They destroyed their letters written during the years between 1870 and 1876 and Jane gave the remaining correspondence to Wilfrid Scawen Blunt for safe-keeping, with the instructions:

'Not to be published until 50 years after my death.'

A RURAL IDYLL

Life by the river was an inexhaustible subject of Morris's writing. Rooks, moorhens, snowdrops, apple blossom, buttercups, willowherb and rose hips – all were described in vivid detail, particularly to his daughter Jenny who, to her parents' distress, was discovered to be suffering from severe epilepsy. He wrote frequently to her, his letters infused with the joy of changing seasons. Of spring, he wrote:

> I have eaten asparagus and heard the cuckoo: the blackbirds wake me about 4 o'clock a.m.: as for the rooks they never stop all day long. I saw a leash of plovers yesterday squawking away, and making believe that they had no nest at hand. The garden is full of bullfinches, which are fat pretty dears, and sing a little short song very sweetly.

Of early summer:

> The fields are all butter-cuppy. The elms are mostly green up to their tops: the hawthorn not out, but the crabs beautiful, and also that white-beam with the umbelliferous flowers ... the cherry tree near the arbour opposite my window is a mass of bloom. The heartseases are beautiful.

Of late summer by the river:

> ... the bank still being very beautiful with flowers; the long purples, and willow-herb ... the purple blossom of the house mint and mouse-ear and here and there a bit of meadow-sweet ...

Morris's correspondence with Georgiana Burne-Jones expresses thoughts and feelings that he would not reveal to anyone else. She was intelligent and strong-minded, second of four formidable daughters of a Birmingham Methodist minister, women whose progeny included the writer Rudyard Kipling and the Conservative Prime Minister Stanley Baldwin. Georgiana was first introduced to Morris when she was fifteen. Years later, their friendship deepened when both were enduring

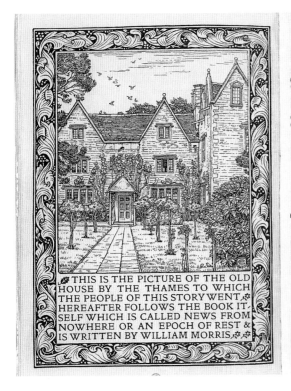

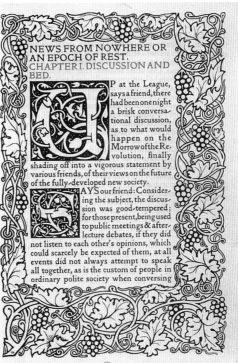

The frontispiece and first page of News from Nowhere. *The frontispiece, drawn by the young Charles March Gere (1869–1957), shows the east front of Kelmscott Manor. Kelmscott is eulogized in* News from Nowhere: *'A house that I love I think . . . so much has the old house grown up out of the soil and the lives of those that lived in it.' When travellers approached Kelmscott they opened a door in the stone outer wall to discover a perfect summer garden: 'The garden between the wall and the house was redolent of the June flowers, and the roses were rolling over one another with that delicious superabundance . . .'*

the infidelity of their respective partners, and Morris came to rely on her judgment, often asking for her opinion on his work. He also formed a close and lasting friendship with Aglaia Coronio, a wealthy member of the Greek community in London and part of the Pre-Raphaelite social circle. She set out to charm Morris at a time when his reputation was growing.

The playwright George Bernard Shaw wrote that it was a positive pleasure to visit Morris's country house – even though he woke one morning to find that the glass of water beside his bed had frozen solid. He described a happy week at Kelmscott with the Morris family in August 1888, rowing and sailing on the river, shooting with bows and arrows, playing hide and seek and quizzing visiting children with 'vegetable, animal or mineral?'

Artists and craftsmen called at Kelmscott Manor for inspiration, particularly after the publication of Morris's novel, *News from Nowhere*, which described the old Elizabethan house and its garden and featured an illustration of the rose-flanked front path. One visitor in 1896, Maud Herapath, who must have come on the servants' day off, described the house as lovely, but

'artistic and grubby'. She was horrified to discover that tea at the home of the great William Morris included a loaf on the table and a jam pot with a sticky spoon: 'we did not accept the tea,' she sniffed, 'but sat in a row in the plain, painfully plain, dining room and stared at Miss Morris and wondered why she dressed in such a sloppy way with no stays.'

Whatever the shortcomings in presentation, the Kelmscott table was laden daily with vegetables from the kitchen garden, and in season there were cherries, strawberries, raspberries, gooseberries, apples and plums. The flowers, too, made an impressive display in summer, and Georgiana wrote that the garden was 'enchanting with flowers, one mass of them, and all kept in beautiful order'.

Plants and trees from Kelmscott were immortalized in Morris's wallpapers and fabrics. He spent hours studying and sketching them before taking the drawings back to his works and weaving them into his patterns. His chintzes of the mid-1870s, such as *Honeysuckle*, *Iris* and *Marigold*, reflect his deep enjoyment of the garden. He collected roots, flowers and willow twigs to

LEFT Design for Windrush, *printed textile, 1883, the first of a series of designs that took their titles from Thames tributaries and other waterways with which Morris had connections: the Cray, Cherwell, Evenlode, Kennet, Lea, Lodden, Medway, Windrush, Wey, Wandle, Avon and Severn. He particularly liked the fact that the same river that ran through meadows near Kelmscott Manor flowed past his London house at Hammersmith.*

RIGHT Cartoon for Vine and Acanthus, *tapestry, 1879, drawn after a design by Morris. Although Morris was firmly of the opinion that classical buildings did not suit the English landscape, this view did not stop him using a classical motif, the acanthus, in his designs. Again, birds are hidden among the foliage.*

make vibrant, true-coloured, vegetable dyes, which he constantly strove to perfect in an age when most textiles were stained with the harsher hues of synthetic, aniline dyes.

In her biography of her father, May Morris described how Morris imparted his knowledge of the countryside to her, even making details of the serrated edges on willow leaves interesting:

> [He] noted every turn of a leaf or attachment of a stem, watched every bird on the wing with keen alert eye: nothing in the open air escaped him.

She added that symbolism in design bored him and that he insisted on observing nature. He designed his most famous wallpaper, *Willow*, after taking a walk with her, enthralling her with the botany of the trees along the river bank. Said May Morris: 'Without being a "symbol" of any special thought, each of the more important patterns for papers or chintz had its mark, its standing, or its bit of story.'

The river beyond the garden was crucial to Morris's pleasure at Kelmscott. He would spend hours in a boat, fishing or watching the birds, or gazing at the meadow plants. Friends noticed that Morris became contented, if rather bossy, when he was on the water. All his life he lived and worked close to the River Thames or its tributaries, and they had a powerful hold on his imagination. He based a series of his designs on these waterways, each with its own references to plants and history.

In his biography of Morris, J.W. Mackail summed up the appeal of Kelmscott to Morris:

> With little bold or striking beauty, it has a charm of unequalled subtlety and lastingness. The young Thames winds through level pastures, among low surrounding hills, in a landscape that seems as if little change had passed over it since the English settlement.

Despite personal sadness, Morris's letters reveal a profound attachment to the place and, over 25 years, he found increasing peace and joy there: 'As others love the race of man through their lovers or their children, so I love the earth through that small space of it.'

FILLED WITH BIRDSONG

Morris's fascination with the changing life of the garden was not confined to the flowers and trees. He particularly loved birds and was admired for his knowledge of their appearance and habits, although he was diffident about his ability to draw them. Mackail records that the blackbirds sang at Kelmscott after they had fallen silent elsewhere; the land between the water and the house was 'always filled with song from a hundred throats'. The linen embroidery on Morris's big four-poster bed at Kelmscott was worked by May with the words of a Morris verse, 'Twixt summer and spring when all birds sing/In the town of the tree . . .'

Morris's letters from Kelmscott constantly refer to the birds: 'As to the garden it seems to me its chief fruit is – blackbirds. However, they have left us some gooseberries, and I shall set to work this morning to get some before their next sit-down meal.' In the late summer of 1871, he wrote:

> The birds were very delightful about us; I have been of late so steeped in London that it was quite a fresh pleasure to see the rooks about, who have been very busy this showery weather. There was no lack of herons in these upper waters, and in the twilight the stint or summer snipe was crying about us and flitting from under the bank and across the stream: such a clean-made, neat-feathered, light grey little chap he is, with a wild musical little note like all the moor-haunting birds.

He mentions herons 'stalking about the fields in the gravest manner'; a kingfisher taking a fish; and a 'sailing' owl. Another letter from Kelmscott Manor describes 'the flowerless autumn garden' and:

> . . . the robins hopping and singing all about the garden. The fieldfares, which are a winter bird and come from Norway are chattering all about the berry trees now, and the starlings, as they have done for two months past, collect in great flocks about sunset, and make such a noise before they go off to roost.

Long before Morris owned a garden, he had pictured birds living in them. In one of his earliest stories, 'Frank's Sealed Letter', Morris describes, 'all the songs of birds ringing through the hedges, and about the willows . . . the tender fresh grass, and the sweet young shoots of flowering things, were very pensive to me . . .' In the closing scene of another early short story, the hero leads his bride home: 'There then shall we be in the garden . . .

63

LEFT Bird, *design for woven cloth, 1877–8. Morris hoped his patterns would bring nature into the house, clothing 'our daily and domestic walls with ornament that reminds us of the outward face of the earth, of the innocent love of animals . . .'*

across the flowers and blending with the voice of the nightingales in the trees . . .' In another story: 'the thrushes perched upon her shoulder, and the hares gambolled together close to the feet of the twain; so that it seemed to them that they had come into the very Garden of God.'

Before his marriage, Morris had visited the zoo at Regent's Park in London to see the large birds. Mackail recounted that, afterwards, he 'would imitate an eagle with considerable skill and humour, climbing on to a chair and, after a sudden pause, coming down with a soft flop'. Many of the heavenly angels of his stained-glass windows are female forms with eagles' wings.

Birds feature more than any other creature in Morris's fabrics, letters, prose and poetry. His first attempt at embroidery included emblematic birds flying near trees, along with the motto 'If I Can'. Made while Morris was still living at Red Lion Square in 1857, the embroidery now hangs at Kelmscott Manor.

Trellis, the first wallpaper designed by Morris and made by the Firm, features birds among the plants. These birds, though, were drawn by Philip Webb. It was fifteen years before Morris managed to use his own drawings of birds in textile designs, writing in a letter to Thomas Wardle in 1877, 'I am studying birds now to see if I can get them into my next design.' Success came with *Bird*, a woven cloth designed the following year – the Firm's first manufactured textile to include a bird motif. This was followed in 1879 by the first tapestry designed and woven by Morris, *Vine and Acanthus* (affectionately known as *Cabbage and Vine*, because the acanthus foliage resembled cabbage leaves), which also includes birds in pairs. More pairs appeared in the pattern for the silk and wool fabric, *Dove and Rose*. Even *Brother Rabbit* is balanced with bird forms, but in the wallpaper *Bird and Anemone* the birds are perched individually on stems. A similar relationship is seen in Morris's carpet, *Bullerswood*. In the *Woodpecker* tapestry, however, the birds are not in a pattern, but form the actual focus of the design.

Strawberry Thief features thrushes, the inspiration for which came from the garden at Kelmscott. May wrote:

You can picture my Father going out in the early morning and watching the rascally thrushes at work on the fruit-beds and telling the gardener who growls, 'I'd like to wring their necks!' that no bird in the garden must be touched. There were certainly more birds than strawberries in spite of attempts at protection.

This attitude shared the sentiments of the fashionable Victorian naturalist Richard Jefferies:

the true gardener will have a thought for the birds. No modern exotic evergreen ever attracts our English birds like the true old English trees and shrubs. In the box and yew they love to build; spindly laurels and rhododendrons, with vacant draughty spaces beneath, they detest, avoiding them as much as possible. The common hawthorn hedge round a country garden shall contain three times as many nests, and be visited by five times as many birds as the foreign evergreens, so costly to rear and so sure to be killed by the first old-fashioned frost.

In his 1881 lecture 'Some Hints on Pattern Designing', Morris talked about 'swallows sweeping above the garden boughs towards the house-eaves where their nestlings are, while the sun breaks on them'. After meeting Morris watching birds in the garden, Wilfrid Blunt wrote that he 'creeps about a little among them in the sun'. On what was to be his last visit to Kelmscott Manor in April 1896, Morris expressed his feeling for gardens and birds in a letter to Georgiana:

I have enjoyed the garden very much and should never be bored by walking about and about in it. And although you think I don't like music, I assure you that the rooks and blackbirds have been a great consolation to me.

During his stay, Morris woke to the dawn chorus and, in his diary, noted that a cuckoo sang for three consecutive mornings at 7am – followed later by the rooks and blackbirds. Until his final days Morris found peace in his gardens. His life and work revealed his consciousness of the interdependence of plants and animals. Like thoughtful gardeners today, he was aware of the part his garden had to play in the cycle of nature.

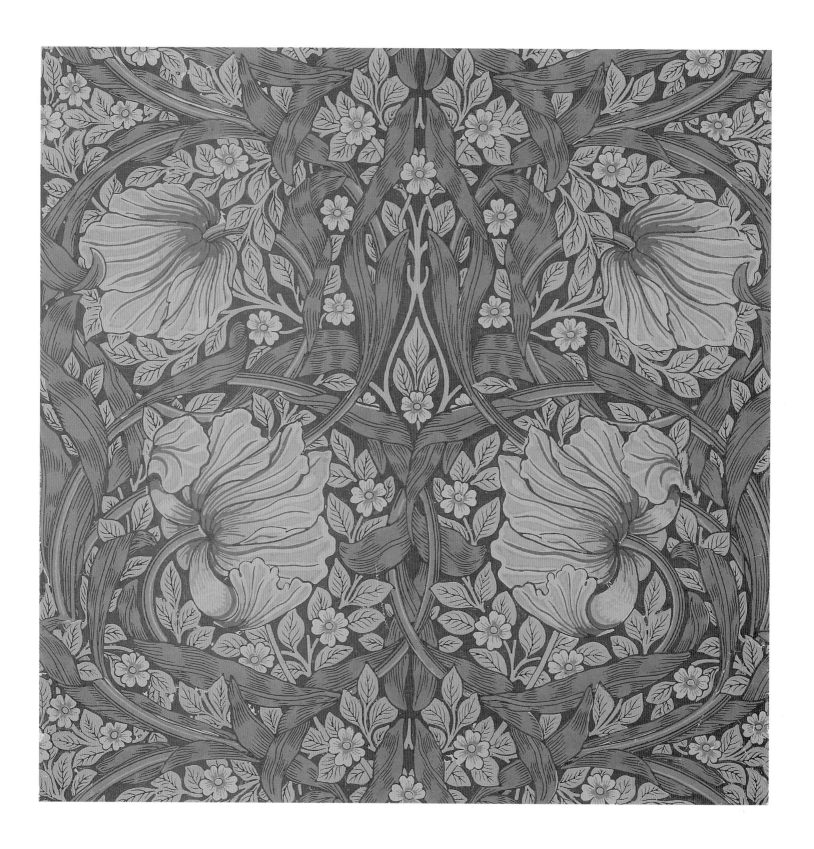

KELMSCOTT HOUSE

THE MID-1870S SAW MAJOR CHANGES in the lives of the Morris family: Jane ceased her affair with Rossetti; F.S. Ellis, Morris's publisher, replaced Rossetti as his co-lessee of Kelmscott; and Morris reorganized the Firm, severing his connection with Rossetti as both a business partner and friend. Morris, with his barely contained energy, was the main driving force in the Firm and he was keen to expand. In 1875 he took sole control, a move not achieved without causing bitterness among some of the other partners. Rossetti even suggested his £1,000 compensation should be given to Jane Morris. The Firm was now renamed Morris & Co.

Although Morris retained a study and a bedroom at Queen Square, the growth of the Firm had led the family to move in 1873 to Horrington House at Turnham Green, west London, 'a *very* little house with a pretty garden', only a few miles from The Grange, the Burne-Joneses' house in Fulham. The close friendship between the Burne-Joneses and Morris – when in London he visited them most Sunday mornings – was reflected in that between their four children. In 1874, Margaret and Philip Burne-Jones and Jenny and May Morris formed a Secret Society in the attic of The Grange, and together they would play out elaborate childish rituals, or climb the garden trees.

But Morris's need for more space for his invalid daughter and for a place fit to show off his furnishings prompted another move to a larger home, Morris's last, on the Upper Mall, overlooking the River Thames at Hammersmith, west London.

When he discovered the large, late-Georgian house in 1875, he saw that it fulfilled his two requirements: water and a garden.

ABOVE A portrait of Morris taken in 1877.

LEFT Pimpernel, *wallpaper, 1876. The dining room at Kelmscott House was hung with this paper.*

The river was so close to the site that at high tide it occasionally flooded the narrow road in front of the house and the garden was large and unspoiled. Once again, it was the garden that proved one of the enticements. In a letter to Jane, who was staying with friends in Italy, Morris wrote:

The situation is certainly the prettiest in London . . . The house could easily be done up at a cost of money. The large drawing-room, with a touch of my art, could be made one of the prettiest in London. The garden is really most beautiful. If you come to think of it, you will find that you won't get a garden or a house with much character unless you go about as far as the Upper Mall. I don't think that either you or I could stand a quite modern house in a street. I don't fancy going back among the bugs of Bloomsbury.

He renamed it Kelmscott House. It was 130 river miles downriver from its namesake in Oxfordshire and Morris listed its attractions: mature elm trees, two arbours, a kitchen garden and a good collection of fruit trees. He divided the garden into three interconnecting parts, rather like the Red House, and each distinct area opened on to another, linked by an encircling gravel walk. Oak planks and neat box hedges were used for borders and boundaries.

Mackail described the garden as long and rambling, with a lawn, an orchard and a kitchen garden, still preserving 'some flavour of the country' among the new buildings that were encroaching on the old, scattered cottages. The passage leading

LEFT The river frontage of Kelmscott House, Hammersmith, c. 1896. The long first-floor drawing room had five windows facing south through tall elms to the river. By the time Morris had decorated the place, he had transformed a rather gloomy, neglected property into a showcase for his finest mature style. George Bernard Shaw called it a 'magical house'. 'Everything that was necessary was clean and handsome: everything else was beautiful and beautifully presented.'

RIGHT The Oxford and Cambridge boat race passing Kelmscott House in 1892. Morris was an enthusiastic host, and boat race day was always celebrated with a party at the house.

from the main road to the garden was called Hog Lane, doubtless a source of amusement, and which may explain the name given to the compost and manure heap at the bottom of the garden – Pig End. Morris took a pride in this area, carefully planting spring-flowering bulbs around the trees. In a letter to his daughter Jenny, he wrote:

> The garden to my cockney eyes is looking pretty well, though I daresay you would think Pig End somewhat dreary; but the new little trees look pretty there and are coming out into bud: I am dissapointed [sic] with the daffies: many of them are blind, some will be quite out in a day or two.

Nearest the house was a wide, smooth lawn shaded by fine, mature trees, among them a weeping ash and a magnificent tulip tree. The lawn became a bowling green for family and friends, and Morris would sometimes take his handmade rugs from the loom in the stables and lay them out on the grass to check the colours in daylight. On either side at the lower end of the lawn

were two leafy arbours. A row of enormous Italian terracotta oil jars, known as the 'Ali Baba pots', were planted with flowing flowers and formed a boundary separating the lawn from the next section. This led the visitor from spacious green to a contrasting area, an orchard, presided over by an ancient mulberry tree and filled with old-fashioned, scented flowers, tall hollyhocks and a riotous mix of herbs and native plants. The last segment was a traditional kitchen garden with a greenhouse, a plentiful supply of raspberries, another old mulberry tree and a collection of fruit trees, including pear and cherry, trained against the walls. A door in the buttressed wall led into Hog Lane. Progress with Morris's plans was slow because the gardener, Matthews, was of an advanced age and Morris refused to replace him with someone younger; and the plans were also often thwarted by cats and poor soil. It could never compete in his affections with his retreat upstream, but to Morris Kelmscott House was a peaceful oasis amid the swirl of London. From his plainly furnished, book-lined rooms on the ground floor he could break from his writing or work on the handloom and find

The Oxford and Cambridge Boat Race 1889

refreshment in the garden among the trees and flowers. On a hot June morning, under a haze of London smoke, he wrote in a letter:

> I have just been down the garden to see how things were doing, and find that they are getting on. Not so many slugs and snails by a long way, and the new-planted things are growing now; the sweet peas promising well, the peonies in bud, as well as the scarlet poppies.

Despite the pressures of his increasingly busy life, Morris still found time to enjoy musical evenings with his daughters and he made two major expeditions up the River Thames from his Kelmscott home in London to the other in Oxfordshire. The first trip, in the summer of 1880, was in a hired boat, *The Ark*, which was crowded with family and friends. Morris was in charge of the cooking and the others watched through the cabin window as he stirred the pot over a spirit stove. The men laughed and joked and played the fool; and a schoolfriend of May's recalled seeing the boat pass under a bridge, Jane sitting in the stern with her embroidery, looking rather wan. The second, equally jolly trip, was made the following summer.

Morris was a devoted father, quite at ease when working with women. In 1885, his talented daughter, May, at the age of 23, became Morris's chief assistant, helping him both with his political work and at Morris & Co., where she was in charge of the embroidery department. It was after a Sunday evening socialist supper at Kelmscott House that George Bernard Shaw, an accomplished charmer, claimed a 'mystic betrothal' to May. This understanding between May and the playwright was so vague that she eventually despaired of a resolution and married someone else. Her choice, to her mother's dismay, was young socialist Henry Halliday Sparling, the slender, immature, son of a farmer. May set up a needlework business at their Hammersmith house, helped, among others, by Lily Yeats, daughter of the poet W.B. Yeats. Unfortunately for Sparling, the embers of the old mystic betrothal were stirred in 1892, when Shaw boldly moved in with the young couple and reignited May's passion. Shaw later left the scene, but by then her marriage was over.

ABOVE *The garden at Kelmscott House today. Morris was delighted when he found Kelmscott House by the Thames at Hammersmith. With its long, rambling garden, it was an oasis for him amid the bustle of London life. After weaving his handmade rugs in the former coach house (to the right of the house in the photograph), Morris would lay them out for inspection on the smooth, wide lawn, shaded by mature trees including a weeping ash and a tulip tree. The grass also became a bowling alley for family and friends. The coach house was later used for socialist gatherings, attended by George Bernard Shaw, W.B. Yeats and Oscar Wilde.*

70

Just weeks before May's divorce was formalized, Shaw married another woman.

PRESERVING THE PAST

Morris's social conscience steered him towards what in his youth would have been a pulpit but was now a public platform. His first crusade was closely attached to his artistic career. Since the age of eight, when he stood awestruck before Canterbury Cathedral, beautiful old buildings had become a vital part of his life and he was distressed to find that many were being ruined by the meddling of insensitive architects. In 1877 Morris, Philip Webb and George Wardle founded the Society for the Protection of Ancient Buildings – SPAB – to preserve the nation's architectural heritage, whether a country church, a cathedral or a farm building and to prevent destruction and mindless restoration. At their general meeting in 1879 he declared:

> . . . every old building is to be regarded as a bequest of the art
> of the past, a bequest which we owe to the art of the future.
> It is not our own property absolutely. We are only custodians
> and trustees . . . our bounden duty is to hand on unimpaired
> to posterity the priceless heritage as we received it.

The Society campaigned for gentle, conservative repair and tried to stop moves to erase the signs of age. Morris travelled the country, constantly checking on planned demolitions and acting to prevent them. He was among the first to make people aware of the importance and beauty of simple rural buildings, such as churches and yeomen's houses, cottages and barns.

The SPAB was motivated by Morris's hatred of the over-restoration of buildings, and one notable international success

ABOVE RIGHT The garden was divided into three spaces. The lawn used for playing bowls was separated from the orchard area by three chest-high terracotta vases.

RIGHT A photograph taken in the garden of The Grange, Burne-Jones's home in Fulham. Morris appears with the four most important women in his life: Jane, his daughters May and Jenny, and Georgiana, Burne-Jones's wife, who became Morris's confidante.

achieved by the Society was that of stopping the proposed 'improvement' of the front of St Mark's Cathedral in Venice. Morris always argued that preserving landscapes and buildings were interrelated activities and it was just as vital to preserve the traditional countryside. In an article in 1899, 'Under an Elm-Tree', Morris wrote:

> The architecture of the Crafts-guildsman will tumble down or be 'restored' for the benefit of the hunters of the picturesque who, hopeless themselves, are incapable of understanding the hopes of past days, or the expression of them. The beauty of the landscape will be exploited and artificialized for the sake of the villa-dweller's purse, where it is striking enough to touch their jaded appetites; but in [some] quiet places . . . it will vanish year by year (as indeed it is now doing) under the attack of the most grovelling commercialism.

The Society's efforts to protect the surroundings of the threatened buildings soon extended to working with open space movements, such as the City Church and Churchyard Protection Society and the Kyrle Society. It even carried out a joint campaign with the Commons Preservation Society and the Metropolitan Public Garden Association to conserve the settings of ancient buildings on village greens. Just before Morris's death, the Society influenced the National Trust, which was formed in 1894, to purchase its first house, the Clergy House at Alfriston in Sussex.

The SPAB is still the largest, oldest and most technically expert national pressure group fighting to save old buildings from decay, demolition and damage. Of all Morris's wide-ranging achievements, the creation of the SPAB can be said, with hindsight, to be one of the most successful and the most long-lasting.

LEFT A copy of Morris's Roots of the Mountains, *printed in 1890 to his order with his choice of type while he prepared to launch his own publishing company, the Kelmscott Press. It was bound at Merton Abbey with the block-printed* Honeysuckle *design, on linen, which shows how the long, curling stems that twine around their neighbours gave the plant its nickname 'woodbine'.*

RIGHT The staff of Kelmscott Press, together with May and William Morris. The Press published finely produced editions of Morris's own works, reprints of English classics and various smaller volumes. Paper was specially made by hand for him in Kent, and he even insisted on organic ingredients in the ink, which came from Germany.

Wm Morris.   May Morris

KELMSCOTT PRESS

In 1891, Morris, now into his fifties, immersed himself in a new craft, founding the Kelmscott Press a few doors away from his Hammersmith house. He mastered the details of paper-making and inks, in addition to designing typefaces and ornamental borders, proving that printing could be art, and once again setting a standard, this time for the owners of the new art presses springing up in Britain, Europe and the United States of America. Morris's books were medieval in style, with their ornamental borders and illuminated letters. The finest and most elaborate of the volumes were the 438 copies of *The Works of Geoffrey Chaucer*, illustrated with 87 engravings after drawings by Burne-Jones and numerous decorations by Morris. Morris regretted that, when he was designing the book, he was unable to fill all the borders with Chaucer's favourite birds.

Kelmscott Press produced 42 titles, for which Morris designed 384 initial letters, 57 borders and 108 half-borders. Apart from his own poetry and prose he published the work of Ruskin and Rossetti, reprints of his favourite books, poems such as *Maud* by Alfred, Lord Tennyson, and English classics.

Ironically, the third book published by Morris was – at the author's own expense – a collection of poems by Wilfrid Blunt. Blunt was Jane's lover at the time. Less than two years after Rossetti's death, she had succumbed to the flattery of the rich explorer and poet who was a compulsive wooer of women among the country-house set. He was pleased to add the great artist's former inamorata to his collection, but his letters reveal true affection for her. Their affair lasted over ten years, until the night Blunt discovered he was too tired to respond to the pansy left in his bedroom at Kelmscott Manor – the signal from Mrs Morris that he should creep along the creaking boards to her room. Blunt was also determined to charm Morris. In fact the two men became friends and Morris stayed on his estate just before he died.

Despite the difficulties throughout most of their married life, Morris and Jane grew closer in later years, sharing a fond concern for one another's health and for the welfare of their daughters, especially the increasingly ill Jenny.

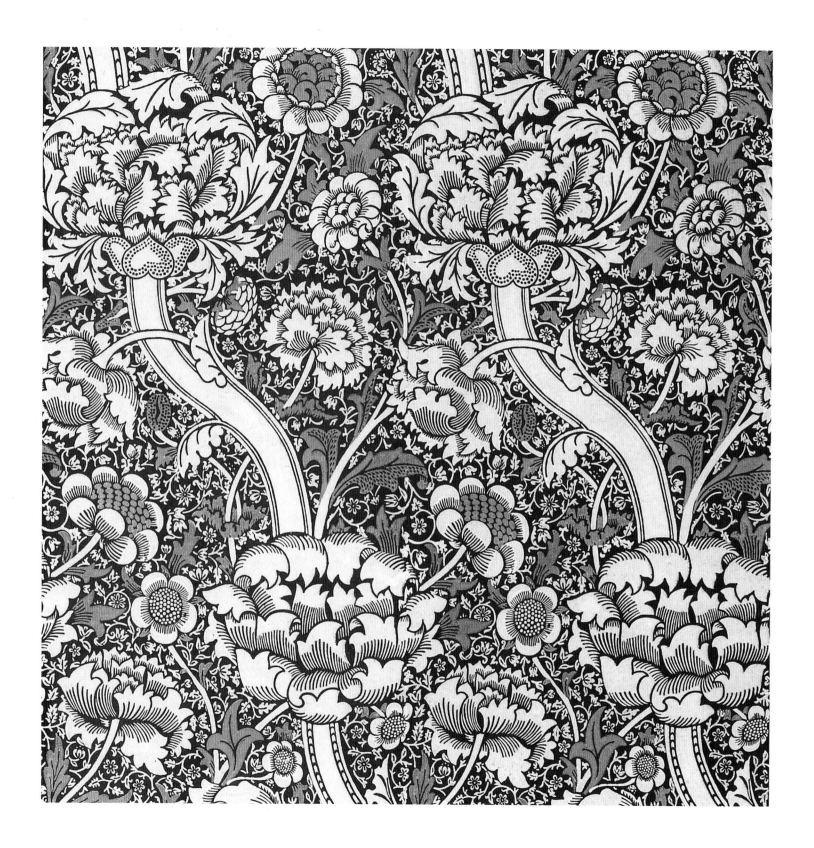

MERTON ABBEY

Morris, like his patterns, was a combination of romance and practicality. He was earning almost £2,000 a year in the 1880s and employing more than 100 workers. Morris & Co. was expanding, with showrooms in a fashionable part of Oxford Street as well as in Manchester, and agents in the United States and Germany. His own appearance contrasted sharply with the immaculate objects he produced. He was often described as scruffy, with a flat and battered soft hat worn on top of unfashionably long, unruly hair. Below the shaggy beard was a burly figure, frequently in a threadbare, blue serge suit with an indigo-dyed shirt of a brighter blue. Even his hands were often blue from indigo dye. It is said that he never looked in a mirror, refusing to have one in his bedroom. Once, rolling down the street with his cloak and satchel, he was taken for a sea captain. On another occasion a servant, startled by his unkempt hair and wild appearance, mistook him for a burglar. When he went to lunch at the house of his friend, Charles Faulkner, the new housemaid thought he was the butcher. According to friends, he seemed to attract dirt while he was working and he often crashed through rooms, knocking things over. From childhood, he had a disconcerting habit of winding his legs so tightly around chair legs as he sat that the frame would sometimes snap.

By the summer of 1881, the company had outgrown Queen Square. Morris could neither live nor work in squalid surroundings, and when it came to choosing new workshops for the company he sought the same beauty he would expect from

ABOVE *Later years: Morris in 1887.*

LEFT Wandle, *fabric design, 1884, named after the river by the model factory Morris opened at Merton in 1881.*

a house. Morris had long wanted premises large enough for him to oversee every aspect of production: the weaving, dyeing and cotton-printing and the making of stained glass. The Cotswolds was his first choice, but it was too far from London, and after a long search he finally found Merton Abbey, a former calico and silk-printing works on the banks of the trout-filled River Wandle in south London, Surrey. The seven acres formed the perfect site, as rustic as it was possible to get so close to the city. Merton bore the Morris hallmarks: historical associations – it had been a priory and Nelson had lived at Merton Place; tradition – Merton had been a centre for textiles; and garden – a neglected but promising cottage garden, fringed with meadows and willows and poplars on the river bank. In spring, the place was carpeted with violets and primroses. The long, low, tarred, weather-boarded sheds with red-tiled roofs were traditional and the Wandle river water was pure and suitable for dyeing. The rushing stream turned the waterwheel and clumps of marsh marigolds glowed on the margins of the millpond, making it a setting fit to inspire some of Morris's finest work.

THE WORKING GARDEN

For Morris and his workers, Merton was a happy release from the cramped, dusty workrooms at Queen Square, and they proved that industry could thrive in a garden setting. One of the first tasks was to restore the garden behind the two buildings that fronted the street. Morris laid a lawn stretching down to the river, planted flowering shrubs and set out a wide border with a mass of old-fashioned flowers,

LEFT *Much of the river by Merton Abbey, just off Merton High Street, is as it was when Morris came in 1881, although his factory no longer exists.*

ABOVE Mill Pond, Merton, *after 1881, by Lexden Lewis Pocock. Morris's factory is beyond the poplars. There was a mill house, a pond, a meadow, an orchard and a vegetable garden. The cottons would be stretched out to dry on the buttercup-studded grass.*

RIGHT *The Thames and its tributaries flowed through Morris's patterns and books. This photograph of Merton and the River Wandle, which runs into the Thames at Wandsworth, was taken in 1913.*

among them wallflowers, larkspur, lilies, irises, hollyhocks and sunflowers. Drifts of daffodils were planted beneath the willow trees. Visitors to the rambling factory were amused to see ducks wandering around. One in 1882 remarked: 'White hawthorn was out in the garden . . . we had tea with Mr. Morris . . . and left laden with marsh marigolds, wallflowers, lilac and hawthorn.' Morris himself used to take great bunches home to Hammersmith, wondering why the sight of a man carrying flowers on the train should be considered comical. In the spring of 1883, less than two years after signing the lease, Morris wrote to his daughter Jenny, describing the beauty of white blossom, the almond tree and the frothy hawthorn:

> the marsh marigolds are all out and are splendid; one clump by the tailside [of the waterwheel] is a picture . . . the apple trees are nearly in full blossom: at Merton, by the way, they are lovely . . . Did you like the flowers I sent you from Axminster by the way? I will pick a big bunch of wall-flowers tomorrow and send them to you . . .

In another letter he wrote:

> Merton is really looking very pretty now, the hawthorn just coming out; but scarce any lilac, there is one pretty blossom-tree which is new to me with white blossoms something like Portugal laurel blossoms: Edgar says it is the Dog-wood, but I can't find it in Gerard.

There was a vegetable garden, which was divided into plots and tended by some of the workers – Merton Abbey even produced its own asparagus – so fulfilling Morris's ideal of a self-sufficient working community. George Wardle, who supervised production, said simply: 'There seems nothing to say except that it was altogether delightful.' So delightful, in fact, that Morris would bring his family to Merton Abbey for celebratory picnics in the garden when a stained-glass window was completed. After touring the works, according to May Morris, they would stand at the foot of a stairway 'looking up at the jewelled beauty of the glass, set up to be examined'.

The idea of bringing the joy of a garden into a factory setting was ingrained in Morris, who had strong views on working

ABOVE Morris's shed for washing chintz in the Wandle. In addition to dyeing cloth, the factory had a stained-glass studio, a glass-firing kiln, a weaving shed, carpet and tapestry looms, a fabric-printing room and a dormitory house for the apprentice boys.

RIGHT Corncockle, chintz, 1883, a clear example of Morris juxtaposing familiar wildflowers with historical patterns. The flower after which the pattern is named appears as if in its field of corn.

conditions. In his essay 'A Factory as it Might Be' (1884), he envisaged pleasant surroundings. Blunt, writing about a visit to Merton in 1892, when he met Morris's brother, Edgar, who had fallen on hard times and worked happily for a weekly wage, said:

> working in the dye vats there, a dreamy man in workman's clothes, with his shirt sleeves turned up, and his arms blue with indigo to the elbows . . . He lives at Merton, and is quite happy, indeed he looked so, dipping wool all day in the vats, in a shed open on to the garden.

Morris's letters constantly referred to the garden. To an American correspondent in 1884, he wrote:

> I was at Merton yesterday, a beautiful spring day and the garden covered with primroses & violets; the daffodils in huge quantities almost out, and a beautiful almond tree in blossom relieved against our black sheds looking lovely.

The French writer Gabriel Mourey toured the Merton works and was impressed by evidence of Morris bringing the natural environment into the life and activities of the workers. He wrote rather floridly of Morris's work:

> . . . this imagination, this power to create, this rare gift of transforming one's subject into seductive harmony of form, happy combination of lines, enchanting rhythms of colour . . . enriching it with one's fancy until it blossoms forth in beauty, melancholy, or merely fresh and simple tones – what other worker in decorative art possesses these to such a degree as he?

The basis of Morris's genius, Mourey surmised, was a sincere study of nature, a thorough grounding in history and a sympathy with his materials. 'One must,' he concluded, 'have lived an English life.'

Before the turn of the century, just after Morris died, Mackail said the works at Merton were still an extraordinary sight:

> . . . as one turns out of the dusty high road and passes through the manager's little house, the world seems left in a moment behind. The old-fashioned garden is gay with irises and daffodils in spring, with hollyhocks and sunflowers in autumn, and full, summer by summer, of the fragrant flowering shrubs that make a London suburb into a brief June Paradise. It rambles away towards the mill pond with its fringe of tall poplars . . . the low long buildings with the clear rushing little stream running between them, and the wooden outside staircases leading to their upper storey, have nothing about them to suggest the modern factory; even upon the great sunk dye-vats the sun flickers through leaves, and trout leap outside the windows of the long cheerful room where the carpet-looms are built.

It is a sadness of modern times, and of the 'progress' Morris so detested, that this idyllic place is now a supermarket car park.

SOCIALISM

Although Morris ran a commerical enterprise, albeit with the help of devoted business managers, his idealism, which had nearly led him into holy orders, now resurfaced as a passionate belief in socialism. This flowed from his strident attacks on the shoddiness of mass production and his belief that workmen, like medieval craftsmen, should have the satisfaction of making individual artefacts. Guilt, perhaps, also played a part. He was well aware of his good fortune in inheriting money while many people endured miserable existences on meagre wages. In a lecture in Staffordshire in 1881, he told how ruffians would sometimes pass the window of his Hammersmith house:

> . . . as I hear the yells, and shrieks . . . as I see the brutal, reckless faces and figures go past . . . fierce wrath takes possession of me – till I remember, as I hope I mostly do, that it was my good luck to be born respectable and rich, that has put me on this side of the window amongst delightful books and lovely works of art, and not on the other side in the empty street, the drink-steeped liquor shop, the foul and degraded lodgings.

Morris's first active political involvement came in 1876, when he joined the campaign against the Disraeli government's alliance with the Turks, despite Turkish atrocities in Bulgaria. Deep disillusionment with the main political parties resulted, prompting an emerging movement among some members of the working classes towards revolutionary socialism.

Hatred of the inequalities of Victorian society led Morris to join the Democratic Federation, later the Social-Democratic Federation. For Jane Morris there was a terrible irony in her husband's new passionate support for the working classes – she had married to escape her working-class background. Now she was threatened with daily contact with the poverty and injustices she thought she had left for ever.

The nascent socialist movement was disorganized, with only a few hundred activists, but Morris plunged himself into radical politics, studying the writings of Karl Marx. Conflicts within the

Federation led to a split, and Morris formed a new, breakaway group, the Socialist League, with Marx's youngest daughter, Eleanor, among the members. They campaigned for better conditions for the working classes, the right of free speech and equality for women. Morris felt, as did Ruskin, that the industrial age had robbed working men of dignity and pride in individual skills and handicrafts. He believed the best way of achieving it was through education – by spreading the word and by integrating politics with art and literature.

Meetings of the Hammersmith branch were held at Kelmscott House in the old coach house, a long, narrow room with a bare board floor and a glimpse of the garden through the window. Political gatherings continued there after the Socialist League had disintegrated, hijacked by anarchists, and the independent Hammersmith Socialist Society had been formed in its place. George Bernard Shaw, a great admirer of Morris as a political thinker, was a regular lecturer there and, at various times, the audience included Oscar Wilde, H.G. Wells, W.B. Yeats and a youthful composer, Gustav Holst. Yeats, a frequent visitor to suppers held after meetings, recalled: 'We sat round a long unpolished and unpainted trestle table of new wood in a room where hung Rossetti's *Pomegranate . . .*'

During these political years, Morris, to the bafflement of most of his friends, took on a different character, tirelessly travelling the country to give earnest lectures, selling socialist journals on street corners, speaking at open-air meetings and risking physical assault by taking part in demonstrations. The socialist revolutionary Friedrich Engels dismissed Morris as a 'sentimental' socialist, but although magistrates usually treated him leniently because he was a gentleman, Morris never flinched when it came to facing the police on a windy street corner. Undeterred by riots and clashes with the authorities, who were often heavy-handed in breaking up socialist meetings, he was once arrested for disturbance, but was later set free and emerged to the cheers of the crowd. He also frequently attended court to stand surety for working-class comrades who were judged more harshly.

Some of his friends were aghast, but Morris believed in action in support of his beliefs. In addition to giving lectures, he edited the Socialist League's journal, *The Commonweal*, and was its chief contributor in both words and funding.

The Rally, *a sketch by Walter Crane, shows Morris, wearing a characteristic blue serge suit and soft felt hat, addressing a May Day socialist gathering at Hyde Park in the 1880s.*

Morris was not a great orator, but his message was heartfelt. A worker described his effect on an audience at Bristol, as he strode on to the platform with his 'massive, lionlike' head and shaggy hair and beard showing traces of grey. During Morris's talk on 'Art and Labour' (1884), the literary folk in the crowd clapped politely, but, said Samson Bryher:

we workmen, somewhat shy and painfully conscious of our unusual surroundings and shortcomings, soon realised the presence of a champion, forgot ourselves, and frequently burst into rounds of applause.

Morris's talks were not always received with such rapture. Once he asked a lady how she had liked his lecture and received the unexpected reply, 'Not at all! But I thought the colour of your blue shirt charming.'

A GUIDING SPIRIT

BY THE LATE 1880S, MORRIS'S ACTIVE INTEREST in politics was waning and he was once more devoting most of his time to creative work. His influence as a master of the decorative arts had spread abroad and his work was followed with particular enthusiasm in Germany and the United States of America. In London, he was such an authority on textiles and embroideries that he was always consulted by the South Kensington museum before it bought such material for the national collections and on one buying trip to Paris, made at very short notice, he even advanced a considerable sum of money to the museum's director.

The Arts and Crafts movement, which had begun with the revival of rural crafts throughout the country, was gaining strength. Architects, silversmiths, weavers, engravers, printers and other artists joined together in a concerted campaign against mass production through the maintenance of high standards and the understanding of the materials of their craft. In 1884, five young architects founded the Art Workers' Guild by merging their society with a group of decorative artists and craftsmen. The aim of the Guild was to break down the barriers between fine and applied arts and to promote simplicity of design. As a champion of their ideas, Morris was elected as an honorary member. Later, some members saw the need for a stronger link with the public and this gave rise in 1888 to the Arts and Crafts Exhibition Society, which, until the First World War, held regular, influential exhibitions of both commercial and amateur

William Morris

ABOVE *Morris in his study at Kelmscott House in the early 1890s.*

LEFT *Detail from* Guiding Spirit, 1869, *stained glass from St Michael's Church, Tilehurst, Berkshire. The flaming stars were a new departure for Morris at a time when he was experimenting with fresh ideas for background settings.*

design. The name 'Arts and Crafts' had been devised by the bookbinder Thomas Cobden-Sanderson, who lived near Morris in Hammersmith.

Absorbed in socialism, Morris was initially cool towards the exhibition project, believing it would not be financially viable and that there was not enough public interest. But once the decision was made to go ahead, he gave his entire support and the first show in London was a great success. Morris himself gave a demonstration of weaving and by 1891, he was sufficiently enthused to take over as president of the Exhibition Society. The year after, he was elected Master of the Art Workers' Guild, which had become the hub of the Arts and Crafts movement.

FINAL YEARS

A life in pursuit of perfection, taken at the gallop, was beginning to undermine Morris's health. Aged beyond his years, he suffered a severe attack of gout in the spring of 1891 from which he never entirely recovered. By 1894, the year his mother died at the age of 90, Morris's health was visibly deteriorating. To his friends' dismay, his prodigious energy slowly dwindled, although he was still writing poetry and working with zeal on the Kelmscott Press books. Diabetes was diagnosed and his weakness led to tuberculosis and kidney problems. In addition, he seemed to be showing some signs of degeneration in his hand and wrist.

During a warm May that year, he and some friends spent an idyllic day walking in his beloved Epping Forest as they talked

LEFT William Morris's funeral cart. His final journey was in this open yellow-painted harvest-cart, festooned with leaves and boughs, and lined with a bed of moss. One of the most eloquent tributes came from the Lancashire Branch of the Social Democratic Federation: 'Comrade Morris is not dead, there is not a Socialist living who would believe him dead for he lives in the heart of all true men and women still and will do so to the end of time.'

RIGHT May Morris at Kelmscott. After her father's death, she continued to live at Kelmscott, where she completed the task of editing his works.

and laughed. Early in 1896, he made his last public speech at the Society of Arts, condemning the rash of advertising posters that were beginning to spoil the countryside.

A cruise to Norway failed to restore his health and he was confined to Kelmscott House with congestion of the lung, tended by family and friends, among them Burne-Jones and his wife Georgiana, Philip Webb and his devoted publisher Frederick Ellis. Jane, May and Georgiana were with him when he died on an October morning that year, 'as quietly as a babe', according to Georgiana. He was 62 years old, exhausted by a life of extraordinary productivity. His doctor said he died from 'simply being William Morris and having done more work than most ten men'. Shaw wrote: 'Happy Morris! he is *resting.*'

Morris had been gifted with the talent to conserve the past while transmuting it into something fresh and original; the courage to act on his belief in radical social reform, while at the same time employing hundreds of workers; and the ability to profoundly alter people's artistic perceptions without starving in a garret, but while making a comfortable living. He was a very English revolutionary.

In a plain oak coffin covered with an antique brocade cloth, Morris's body was taken by train from Paddington Station in London to Lechlade. It was met by a yellow open harvest-cart with red wheels, decorated with vine leaves and willow boughs, and lined with a bed of moss. In drenching rain, the cortège made its way to Kelmscott Church, with Morris's widow, Jane, white and shaking, and his daughter Jenny sobbing helplessly. At the simple ceremony held among glistening wet gravestones, villagers in their working clothes stood alongside artists, socialists and workmen from Merton Abbey, a grieving Burne-Jones and other surviving friends from Oxford. Morris was buried in the south-east of the churchyard, beneath a roof-shaped stone tomb carved with trees, designed for him by Webb, the architect of his first house.

AFTER MORRIS

Jane and May Morris spent the winter at Sheykh Obeyd, outside Cairo, with Wilfrid Blunt and his wife. Jane gave up the lease on the Hammersmith house, settling at Kelmscott Manor, where Jenny mostly stayed too, looked after by a nurse. Jenny would wander round the garden, hoping, she said, to meet her dear father. Jane spent the winters either in London, or with Morris's widowed sister, Emma, at Lyme Regis, Dorset. In 1913, a year before she died, Jane bought Kelmscott Manor for £4,000.

May, who had reverted to the name Morris after her divorce in 1899, became a leading craftswoman herself, designing and producing fine embroideries, writing articles and a book, *Decorative Needlework* (1893). Managing her own group of embroiderers, she founded the Women's Guild of Art and established a wider reputation by teaching and lecturing in Great Britain and the United States. After a doomed affair with New York lawyer John Quinn, May settled contentedly at Kelmscott Manor with a sturdy, crop-haired companion, former land-girl Mary Lobb. May took on the huge task of preserving her father's writings – a massive 24 volumes – and building a memorial hall to him at Kelmscott. Jenny Morris died in 1935 and, following May's death three years later, the house was left in trust to Oxford University. Today it is maintained by the Society of Antiquaries.

When Morris died, a review in the influential arts and interior design magazine *The Studio* predicted that Morris's insistence on quality and on innovation would inspire a future generation:

> Looking at the beautiful objects which his enterprise had made possible one felt that although the master had been taken, the principles he had established were so firmly rooted that the legend of William Morris would be the creed of the new movement and loyal adherence to his teaching would rank more than ever as its watchword.

ABOVE LEFT Gertrude Jekyll aged 80 in the Spring Garden at Munstead Wood, her home in Surrey. She was a designer-craftsman in the Morris mould, an artist, embroiderer, silver-worker and interior decorator. When she turned to gardening, she, like Morris, made a thorough study of her materials – plants. She had her own plant nursery, contributed regularly to William Robinson's The Garden, and was gardening correspondent for Country Life.

ABOVE William Robinson – like Ruskin and Morris – condemned the cult of the hothouse and bedding-out, favouring simple cottage plants.

LEFT Mixed Flower and Vase pattern by Gertrude Jekyll, who also used her decorative embroidery designs on the title pages of her books, shows similarity with her garden designs – a profusion of flowers subtly contained within controlled lines.

THE DISCIPLES

Morris's work in interior decoration has indeed remained popular to the present day. Less well appreciated are the sentiments that strongly influenced a new direction in gardening: his love of a lush profusion of natural-looking flowers and of native trees; his delight in the delicate simplicity of flowers, such as the dog-rose; his loathing of garish bedding plants; and his interlacing of English and exotic in the garden. The iconoclastic gardener and writer William Robinson, author of *The English Flower Garden* (1883), the seminal garden designer Gertrude Jekyll and John Sedding, author of *Garden Craft Old and New* (1891), all owe him a debt.

Morris's dazzling versatility in mastering so many different crafts made a deep impression on a quick-witted, rather plain young woman who was studying painting in South Kensington. She was Gertrude Jekyll, the eighteen-year-old daughter of well-to-do parents, who was destined to become one of the most potent forces in the evolution of the English garden.

Miss Jekyll had already imbibed the teachings of the scourge of Victorian materialism, Ruskin, and, indeed, she moved in the same social circle. But Morris, nine years her senior, was turning Ruskin's ideals into action. Inspired by his work, she too began to experiment with a range of skills: embroidery, wood-carving, silverwork, gilding and interior decoration, searching as Morris did for the perfect creative outlet.

She met Morris at Queen Square in 1869 and years later, in the publication *National Review*, she paid tribute to the 'enormous influence he has had in the education of public taste'. After the meeting she concentrated on textiles and embroidery, becoming a skilled needlewoman and winning commissions from Lord Leighton and the Duke of Westminster. A close interest in Morris's patterns may be responsible for her acute sense of colour and design, and her regard for native flowers. Her own floral designs of the time owed more to Morris than to anyone else. In some aspects the two characters were alike, doggedly following their own star, stoically suppressing displays of emotion and working obsessively, despite having independent means. Jekyll shared Morris's mystical feeling for nature, dating, she said, from the age of about seven when she suddenly came upon a glorious cluster of primroses in a Surrey wood.

Morris may have been the guiding spirit behind Miss Jekyll's gardens, but it was she who spent years of hard work building on his theories and through her own vision she made them triumphantly real. She was responsible for bringing gardening into the Arts and Crafts movement. In her book *Roses for English Gardens* (1902), she describes their ideal, which was based on Morris's yearning for a return to the integrity of the cottage plot:

> the blend of old yew hedges, the cottager's instinctive topiary, herbs and sundials, apple trees festooned with roses and flower borders filled to overflowing with simple, old-fashioned flowers.

Miss Jekyll perfected many of Morris's precepts: combining order and wildness; contrasting a structured framework with exuberant planting of cottage-garden flowers that scrambled over arches and trailed from stone walls; using a mix of hardy exotics and native plants; and respecting the different areas of a garden while forming a harmonious whole.

The devotion to plants and planting of this intelligent, energetic woman, who often covered her portly form with rough gardening clothes and a blue linen apron, its pocket stuffed with gardening tools, was reinforced by her friendship with that other great figure in turn-of-the-century gardening, the fiery Irishman William Robinson. He too had undoubtedly been encouraged in his strong views by Morris, prefacing *The English Flower Garden* with part of a Morris lecture condemning carpet bedding. Robinson was a sworn enemy of what he referred to as a 'false and hideous' practice. A professional gardener, he became head of the herbaceous section of the Botanic Society's gardens in Regent's Park, London, where there was a small collection of native plants. By looking after these, and touring the countryside for ideas and replacements, Robinson developed a keen interest in indigenous plants and their use in traditional cottage gardens.

Robinson marshalled this knowledge to write *The Wild Garden*, published in 1870, in which, in his irascible way, he fired a blast at contemporary gardens and urged readers to see the merits of planting at least a proportion of indigenous flowers, lamenting, 'The passion for the exotic is so universal that our own finest plants are never planted.' His aim was to prove that a mix of native and old-established, imported hardy plants could be grown in natural, irregular drifts to make a rich, easily maintained garden. Both wild and formal could be combined, he said, with, for example, wild roses used in flower gardens and shrubberies or scrambling over fences.

William Robinson never worked from paper plans, but believed in the importance of adjusting each garden to its site. Stereotypical Victorian gardens, taken from the architect's drawing board and popped into a suburban plot without regard for its locality, were the object of Robinson's wrath. 'What is the use of Essex going into Dorset merely to see the same thing done in the home landscape or the garden?' he wrote in *The English Flower Garden*; 'if Essex were to study his own ground and do the best he could from his own knowledge of the spot, his neighbour might be glad to see his garden.' He raged against horticultural fancies: geometrically shaped beds were 'absurd'; artificial fountains, a 'hideous extravagance'; lack of understanding of plants, 'imbecility'.

Nature and naturalness, economy and simplicity were his watchwords and, like Morris, he harboured a preference for wide, herbaceous borders filled with permanent, natural-looking plants, and bulbs naturalized in grass. In the course of his long life (he died in 1936 at the age of 97), Robinson's pen became busier than his spade. In addition to his popular books, he founded and edited the magazines *The Garden* and *Gardening Illustrated*. The profits from his hard work and enterprise enabled him to buy Gravetye Manor in Sussex, where he lived and gardened for 50 years.

Gertrude Jekyll shared much of Robinson's philosophy and they became friends in the 1870s. Gardening gradually took precedence over her other crafts, possibly because of increasing myopia, or perhaps because she had found her life's work. It became a passion, particularly after creating her own garden at Munstead Wood in Surrey. Jekyll wrote regular articles for William Robinson's publications, proving to be a fluent, persuasive advocate for a natural style of planting. As Elizabeth David did later for cookery, Jekyll whetted the public appetite for gardening. Taking Morris's line, Jekyll believed the first step should be to examine the surrounding countryside before making a garden that was in complete harmony with its site. 'No artificial planting can ever equal that of nature,' she wrote in her book *Wood and Garden* (1899), 'but one may learn from it the great lesson of moderation and reserve, of simplicity of intention, and directness of purpose . . .'

The main rooms of her house at Munstead Wood opened on to a natural clearing surrounded by graceful, mature birch trees. Colours, carefully grouped and graded, were important in her gardens and she planted with a painter's eye, selecting colour and form to adapt to the seasons and changing light. The artless effect was achieved only with some sophistication; she explained her methods in the chapter on colour schemes she wrote for *The English Flower Garden*.

A chance meeting in the spring of 1889 with the 20-year-old architect Edwin Lutyens, 25 years her junior, led to a second, inspired partnership, which brought them both worldwide renown. They shared a love of Surrey, with its old, tile-hung cottages and simple, mixed gardens, and together they would trot along the lanes in her cart, making detailed notes on old local buildings and their gardens. These images, according to Mavis Batey in *Gertrude Jekyll – Essays on the Life of a Working Amateur*, were assimilated into Jekyll's designs: 'lavender and hollyhocks by an old weather-boarded barn, snapdragons along a brick wall, cottage porches wreathed with roses, ferns in

LEFT *The Terrace at William Robinson's house, Gravetye Manor. In addition to his naturalistic woodland gardening, Robinson introduced formal elements near the Elizabethan house. A shrewd businessman, he had bought the Gravetye estate in Sussex in 1885. Here he was able to put his gardening ideas into practice. His book* The Wild Garden *promoted gardening with naturalized plants, turning away from architectural garden design. That same year he had launched* The Garden, *a periodical that soon became influential and frequently quoted Ruskin and Morris.*

RIGHT *Munstead Wood: the Fern and Lily Walk led from Gertrude Jekyll's house (built for her in the vernacular style by Edwin Lutyens) to the Surrey woodland beyond. She had met Morris and shared both his sense of belonging to a particular patch of earth and the idea that a house and garden should partake of 'the continuous life of the earth'.*

dipping wells, reflections, patterns of brick and ironstone or millstones set in garden paths'. Lutyens and Jekyll showed 'William Morris's capacity for looking at the traditions of the past with a fresh eye'. Between them, they realized some of the finest marriages ever made between house and garden.

Miss Jekyll continued to write her own books, reiterating the lessons of Ruskin and Morris. Her intensely felt bond with a special piece of land mirrored Morris's and when her family moved to Berkshire for eight years she so missed the sunken lanes and leafy woods of Surrey that she described it as a painful exile. This respect for locality recurs throughout her writing and in *Gardens for Small Country Houses* (1912) she confirms the importance of respecting the individual characteristics of a site. Referring to a hilly, moorland setting, she writes:

> There are natural gardens in these places, and especially natural groves, that cannot be bettered in the way of consistent and harmonious planting by any choice from a nursery catalogue. Such a region . . . is clothed with juniper, holly, birch, mountain ash, scrub oak and Scotch fir, in delightfully spontaneous grouping, with undergrowth of bracken and whortleberry, and heaths in the more open places, and other delights of honeysuckle, wild thyme, wood sage and dwarf scabious. It is grievous to see this natural and well-adjusted beauty ruthlessly destroyed, and common nursery stuff, such as laurels and a heterogeneous collection of exotic conifers, put in its place, whereas it may be so well planted with the native trees that are absolutely sympathetic to its own character.

Each area, she said, has its own flora 'indicating to the careful observer the classes of trees and plants that will best flourish and best adorn', and to these could be added plants such as brooms, rosemary, lavender or phlomis.

She continues Morris's warnings about the 'disastrous' effect of imported conifers in gardens:

> . . . it is safer to trust our native evergreens and the few European kinds that we have long known. In their way nothing is better than our native juniper, Scotch fir and yew for our sandy uplands; yew also, for chalky soils, and spruce and silver

fir for cool hollows. Our noble English yew is nearly always beneficial in the garden landscape. Whether as a trimmed hedge or as a free-growing tree, its splendid richness of deepest green, and, indeed, its whole aspect, is of the utmost value.

Gertrude Jekyll's deep regard for nature led her to recommend native plants wherever they were most fitting in a garden; she loved the combination of light, delicate silver birch and dark, dense holly; she warned against rooting all ivy out of the garden and believed it should be allowed to grow moderately. Even when she was into her eighties, Gertrude Jekyll continued to promote the use of indigenous flora in gardens. Writing to Edwin Lutyens's daughter, Ursula, in 1924 she suggested for the Quarry Garden at Blagdon, Northumberland:

> Birch and green holly here again would be excellent and one or two rambling roses swinging about but only those of the wildish sort. Another capital thing for this sort of use is the wild *clematis vitalba*.

In his modest garden at West Wickham, Kent, John Dando Sedding, the ecclesiastical architect, would often arrive home from work, greet his wife and children, then set to with trowel and hoe in the garden. He and Morris had met while training at G.E. Street's architectural practice. Initially, Sedding's own office was next door to the Firm at Queen Square, and he later moved to premises above Morris's shop in Oxford Street. As a practical gardener, he did much to advance Morris's theories among followers of the Arts and Crafts movement.

Naturally for an architect, he favoured formal gardens, but he shared Morris's respect for old-fashioned flowers and well-filled borders, as well as his distaste for weird geometric beds cut into lawns. Sedding, too, stressed the importance of deferring to local surroundings. In his book, *Garden Craft Old and New*, published after his death in 1891, he wrote:

> The art of gardening is not intended to supersede Nature . . . There is an unerring rightness both in rude Nature and in garden grace, in the chartered liberty of the one, and the unchartered freedom of unadjusted things in the other. Blessed be both!

Kellie Castle, a derelict but unaltered seventeenth-century house in Fife, Scotland, was acquired and restored by James Lorimer, a lawyer. His son Robert planned the gardens as 'a plesaunce' and, like those at Kelmscott Manor, there were enclosed hedged compartments with archways of yew, rose trellises and flower borders edged with box.

He quotes with approval the theories of Sir Gardner Wilkinson, whose book *On Colour* (1858) included a section on native flowers: 'Common flowers,' wrote Wilkinson, 'the weeds of the country, are often most beautiful in colour, and are not to be despised because they are common; they have also the advantage of being hardy, and rare flowers are not always those best suited for beds.'

True to the ethos of the Arts and Crafts movement, Sedding emphasized the importance of garden craft in even the humblest patch of ground:

> In gardening, as in other matters, the true test of one's work is the measure of one's possibilities. A small, trim garden, like a sonnet, may contain the very soul of beauty. A small garden may be as truly admirable as a perfect song or painting.

THE LEGACY

Not long after completion of the Red House garden, Lady Louisa Egerton restructured the grounds at Hardwick Hall in Derbyshire, dividing the area inside the Elizabethan stone walls into four parts with hornbeam and yew hedges. She laid out wide grass walks and a croquet lawn surrounded by evergreens; close to the house she planted a mixed fruit and nut orchard, and in the final section, a vegetable garden. There were wide herbaceous borders planted with perennials and rambling roses, and clematis climbed over old stone walls. By taking the elements of medieval and cottage gardens that Morris so admired and elevating them to a grand country house setting in such a skilful way, Lady Louisa gave the old-fashioned garden the seal of respectability.

Further south at Huntercombe, Buckinghamshire, the Hon. Mrs Evelyn Boyle began redesigning her garden along similar lines in 1871, the year Morris took the lease of Kelmscott Manor. Mrs Boyle did much to popularize the traditional cottage garden and in her writing eleven years later she described high, trimmed hedges of yew and beech; borders filled with old-fashioned

plants; a lavender border; green walks; and a woodland plantation.

Scottish gardeners, too, were inspired to make gardens that built on Scottish tradition. Robert Lorimer, later to become Sir Robert, was only sixteen when, in 1880, he drew his first plans for the garden of his home at Kellie Castle, near Pittenweem, Fife, in which Morris's tenets were already apparent. The outcome was a romantic garden, surrounded by stone walls as shelter from the wind, with a yew alley, fruit and vegetables planted among the flowers, and grass walks edged with box to divide them from borders crammed with bold sweeps of simple flowers. Masses of roses, many of them Scotch briars, clambered over arches and walls, through the fruit trees and in between the border plants.

Lorimer's most important contribution to the Arts and Crafts garden, however, was the transformation of a potato field at Earlshall Castle, eleven miles from Kellie. From 1892, here the London-trained architect worked to create a setting for the severe, grey stone castle that was strict, yet seductive and wholly in keeping with its surroundings. He developed a sequence of interconnecting spaces; clipped holly and yew hedges with a topiary lawn; and a long yew walk, enclosing bays planted with delphiniums, phlox, irises and lilies, leading to a stone arbour. Overflowing flower beds bordered a croquet lawn, rambling roses grew over the walls and, on one side of the terrace, he made an orchard with straight grass paths.

Another architect took Morris's theories and moulded them not to country house or castle, but to the smaller suburban garden. He was Hugh Baillie Scott, who proposed in his book *Houses and Gardens* (1906) that the function of a garden was to grow fruit and vegetables for the household and provide outdoor apartments for the family in fine weather. Like Morris, he looked back to rural simplicity. He did not even hold with the separation between kitchen and ornamental – in fact he suggested that scarlet runner-bean flowers might be used in place of red geraniums.

Baillie Scott also liked mystery and surprises in a garden: wells and pergolas; hazel and willow plantings; shaded grass walks with vistas and stone steps; and walls smothered with climbers. He used to take flowers and twigs of native trees from the garden to his office and draw them in detail, using them as decorative motifs in his houses. 'We can hardly do better,' he wrote, 'than to try and reproduce some of the beauties of the Old English Gardens with their terraces and courts and dusky yew hedges which make such a splendid background to the bright colours of flowers.'

He followed Morris's socialist ideals by designing houses for the new garden cities. Believing that everyone should have a garden, Morris wrote: 'Suppose people lived in little communities among gardens and green fields, so that you could be in the country in five minutes' walk, and had few wants.' The ideal of a garden city was later developed by other altruists into Port Sunlight, Welwyn, Hampstead Garden Suburb and Letchworth. Each of the small, terraced houses built at Hampstead Garden Suburb in 1908 had a carefully planned garden with a straight, tree-lined path to the front door and, at the rear, a terrace, a lawn, ponds and a pergola.

The heyday of the Arts and Crafts gardens came to an end with the First World War, when energies and money were diverted to the fight. In the years between the wars, many gardens sadly fell into neglect and vanished. But the dream of a true, indigenous garden put forward by Morris in his lectures, his patterns and at his own homes had by then become a living entity in forward-looking country estates and suburban plots throughout the kingdom. His ideals emerged at Hidcote Manor in Gloucestershire and at Sissinghurst in Kent, the latter said to be a fusion of Harold Nicolson's classical mind and Vita Sackville-West's romantic heart. The garden was designed with different 'rooms'; a lime walk and a nut walk; cottage-garden flowers; careful use of colour; and exuberant, informal planting. Many of the concepts that had seemed so revolutionary in that far-off Red House era were also incorporated quite naturally into ordinary gardens. In fact, Morris continues to influence leading garden designers today, largely through the work of his greatest propagandist, Gertrude Jekyll.

Proof of the foresight in his garden principles is the quickening pace around the world today of the trend towards natural gardening. Some distance in time and place from those simple flowers in a Kent orchard, Morris's ideals continue to reverberate in Australia and the United States of America, for example, where his plea to preserve the landscape has been readily accepted. Native plants in particular – which need no artificial chemicals to flourish, survive with little water, feed wild creatures and satisfy the senses – have come to be appreciated. Increasingly, gardeners perceive what Morris preached: that a garden should be a provider of food; a source of pleasure; and a part of nature's greater whole.

A carving of Morris in the Home Mead, by George Jack, on the Morris Memorial Cottages, 1902, designed by Webb and given as a legacy to the village by Jane Morris.

THE PLANTS
OF
WILLIAM
MORRIS

The plants described in the pages that follow are the native ones that Morris included in his designs, those which he wrote about in his prose, poetry and letters, or which are known to have been part of his gardens.

Morris was passionate about preserving the ancient landscape. The native flora, such as oak, beech and hornbeam, and the mellow old buildings, especially simple barns and village churches, were the very making of a place, giving an area its individual character. But the uniqueness of the countryside was, he feared, being eroded by the spread of new houses and the tide of mass-produced goods. Even gardens, parks and woods were being filled with fashionable exotics flowing from hothouse production lines. Throughout his writing he insisted that modern life needed the 'virtues of honesty and simplicity'. In an article in William Robinson's *The Garden* (April 1879), stressing the importance of traditional crafts and antiquity, Morris wrote that 'the palaces of kings and lords' differed 'only in size from the little grey church that still so often makes the commonplace English landscape beautiful'. Similarly, in his lectures he tried to steer gardeners away from what he saw as the vulgar fad for ever-more grandiose blooms. He loved simple flowers and in his own designs and gardens many of the plants were those same species which had survived little changed since before Stone Age farmers learned to sharpen their flints.

Scarlet poppy, white campion and grasses grow wild on the roadside verges near Kelmscott in Oxfordshire, a glimpse of unchanged countryside which Morris fought hard to preserve.

Today, alas, Morris's plea to respect simplicity has largely gone unheeded, and most gardens are dominated by imported plants and ornate cultivars. Apart from holly and yew, the plants of hedgerows and woods contribute relatively little to gardens. As well as conveying the sense of place so important to Morris, native plants have adapted over thousands of years to suit the local soil, climate, altitude and the complex web of animals whose survival depends on them. Some plants have evolved differently and are so attuned to locality that in different regions certain strains of birch, hawthorn or dog rose, for example, may vary minutely in chemical composition and come into leaf according to their inherited genetic clocks.

The horticultural pursuit of the dramatic, the 'new' and the long flowering can incur a high price – sterility. Pollinating insects often find it impossible to gather food from altered flowers. But finding unimproved species in nurseries and garden centres may be difficult and there is often confusion about the difference between indigenous and naturalized plants. (A native or indigenous plant is one that has arrived in a country without the intervention of man, whereas a naturalized plant is an introduced exotic that has escaped from cultivation to establish itself in the wild, frequently upsetting the ecological balance in the process.) Most native plants can be grown from seed at home. Propagating them oneself fits in with Morris's ideals of a a return to the simplicity of old methods, in which much is done manually with physical exertion, as given in *The Garden*:

To plough the earth, to cast the net, to fold the flock – these, which are rough occupations enough, and which carry with them many hardships, are good enough for the best of us …

Unlike most plants on sale, native plants have been reproducing themselves for millennia, without the help of man, glasshouses or chemicals. The form and needs of their seeds are diverse: willow seeds are tufted and float on the wind; scabious seeds rely on birds scattering them in their droppings; poppy seeds will germinate 80 years after being gathered, while acorns have a dramatically short shelf-life. Plants grown from seed are biologically superior to those reproduced vegetatively from cuttings, runners or divisions, which are clones and genetically identical to the parent. Like all clones, they carry the same weaknesses and virtues as the parent plant, including any viruses. In contrast, a seed creates an entirely new plant and can throw back to a variety of characteristics.

Plants are not as damaged by inbreeding as animals, but a wide genetic pool is still desirable. To retain broad genetic diversity, collectors with conservation in mind usually take seed from several plants and from different places at least a hundred metres or yards apart. Local eco-types – plants grown from locally sourced seed from plants that have evolved in the vicinity – are generally accepted as the best, but there is often disagreement as to what constitutes a local area because it depends on soil types, drainage and altitude.

Many seeds in the wild have an extended survival strategy, some taking two or three years to germinate. Having a proportion of seeds germinating each year increases a plant's chances of success. Complex 'biological clocks' measure their external environment, including light and moisture. The seeds of many European native plants are set to receive a sequence of warm autumn (late-summer ripening), cold winter (vernalization), and spring warmth, before they germinate.

The seed of wild plants is not as uniform as commercial seedstock, so it is prudent to divide each batch, sowing half in trays or pots and keeping the rest in a refrigerator for planting in spring. After sowing cover the seeds with polythene or glass and keep them in a cold greenhouse, or indoors in an electrically heated propagator or on a window-sill. Once they have germinated, prick out the seedlings as soon as they can be handled.

While Morris promoted the beauty of simple native flowers, he also used cottage-garden flowers and exotics, such as the scarlet runner bean, sunflower, tulip, marigold, snowdrop, passion flower, Madonna lily, jasmine, and apple and other fruit trees. Just as his patterns display the honeysuckle alongside the crown imperial and the cultivated rose with the yew, so it is possible to enhance a garden by mixing understated yet vigorous plants with bolder exotics, gradually interweaving the local flora into an existing garden. By responding to Morris's appeal to respect true, simple plants, gardeners will discover fresh visual delights and gain satisfaction from restoring natural balance to their patch of earth.

A stand of pollarded hornbeams (Carpinus betulus) *(see page 107).*

ALISMA PLANTAGO-AQUATICA & WATER-PLANTAIN (ALISMATACEAE)

RIGHT Alisma plantago-aquatica

BELOW Eyebright, *printed cotton, 1883. Morris used the motifs of common water-plantain and eyebright, to create this relatively simple design. As he once said in a lecture, he 'couldn't do' without 'unmistakable suggestions of gardens and fields, and strange trees, boughs, and tendrils' to make his patterns.*

MORRIS USED THIS aquatic perennial in his textile design *Eyebright*. With its broad, oval plantain-shaped leaves and small pinkish-white flowers borne on tall, over 1m (3ft), erect branching stems, it is 'one of the striking water's edge plants' so loved by Morris. The flowers, which appear mid- to late summer, open in the afternoon. Small flat fruits are produced in autumn.

Like the water-lily, the water-plantain is a plant of still, or slow-moving waterways, and was once common in the wet meadows and ponds of the Thames Valley where Morris lived. Useful for the edge of a pond or stream in either a sunny or partially shaded position, it thrives wherever there is shallow water. It may be raised from seed, kept damp in a loamy compost, but is best propagated by the careful division of its large, leafy clumps. It self-seeds prolifically and can choke a small mud-lined pond if left unchecked.

Many insects visit this plant for its nectar, especially bees and hoverflies. Bees also enjoy the abundant pollen.

ANAGALLIS ARVENSIS & SCARLET PIMPERNEL (PRIMULACEAE)

THIS PRETTY, star-shaped flower was used by Morris in his wallpaper *Pimpernel*. It is named after the common form which is bright red, but blue-petalled varieties sometimes occur, and Morris may have used one of these as his source. The Scarlet Pimpernel became internationally famous in 1905 with Baroness Orczy's novel, where the daring hero left the flower as his enigmatic calling card.

Because the flowers open and close with almost clockwork precision, it was called 'poor man's weather glass' or 'shepherd's sundial'. The petals are light-sensitive: in fine weather the flowers open at about 8am and close about 3pm; but in dull or wet weather they stay firmly shut.

Usually an annual, but sometimes a longer-lived small herb, it grows close to the ground, with neat, quadrangular stems about 5–7.5cm (2–3in) high, and spreading to about 38cm (15in). Even then, it can be overlooked, until its bright flowers open in the sun, contrasting with its mat of clear green foliage.

Robust and decorative, the many-branched scarlet pimpernel is known as a weed of cultivated land, fields, waste ground and dunes. It is sometimes grown as a garden plant and is effective in sunny borders. Propagate by sowing fresh seed or by transplanting naturally occurring seedlings while they are still small.

ABOVE Anagallis arvensis

LEFT Detail from Pimpernel, *wallpaper, 1876. Although Morris probably named this after the small blue pimpernel, botanically the flower is more like the greater stitchwort.*

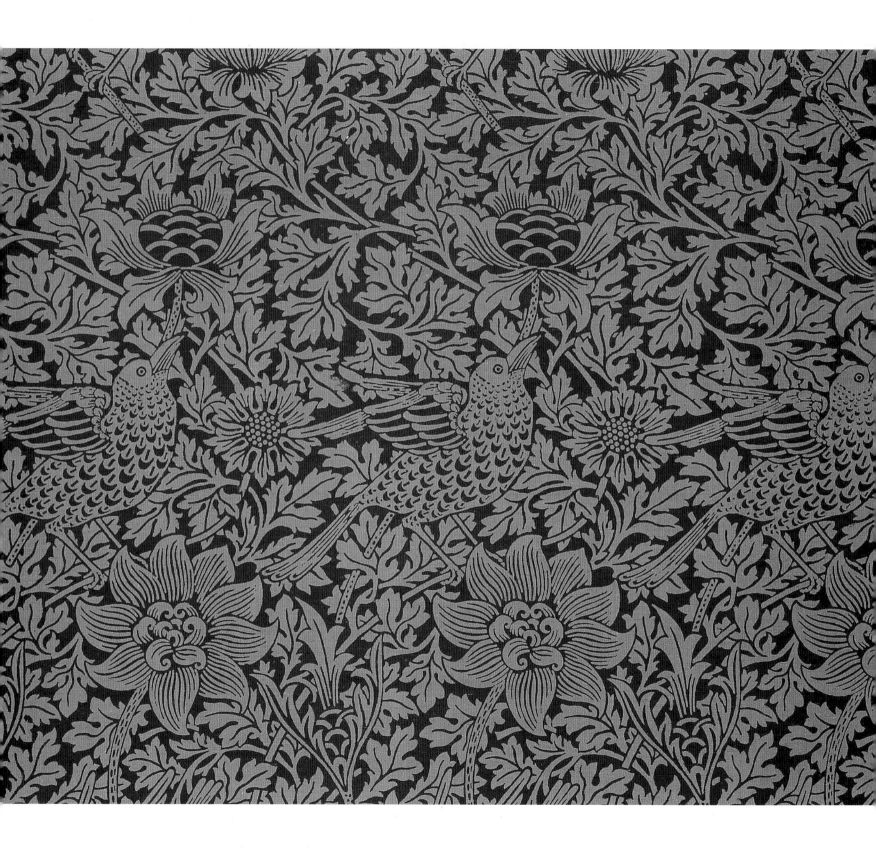

ANEMONE NEMOROSA ❦ WOOD ANEMONE (RANUNCULACEAE)

WITH ITS DELICATE white blossoms and ferny foliage, this charming resident of woods and coppices is an early spring-flowering species and one of the most beautiful. Its kind is celebrated by Morris in his fabric design *Bird and Anemone*. The plant disappears underground in summer, when leafy woods are at their darkest, and it is often a delightful surprise when it appears in spring. It bears single large flowers on slender 10–15cm (4–6in) stems above attractive divided leaves. It is usually white, but some colonies have purple or purple-streaked petals. Many of the anemones seen in woods today are, in fact, garden escapees including *A. apennina*, *A. blanda* and *A. ranunculoides*. Although widespread, wood anemones are usually confined to specific ancient localities of oak and birch.

Well-drained and fertile soil suits this anemone and, in a sunny or partially shaded position, its twig-like rhizomes will spread rapidly to form clumps up to 60cm (24in) or more across. Ideal as an early flower in a sunny border, it is a good understorey to later-flowering plants and may also be planted near deciduous trees and shrubs where, mimicking its natural woodland habitat, it forms white carpets in spring. Propagation is by division of the rhizomes in late summer, or by taking young rooted shoots in early spring.

Although the wood anemone produces no nectar, the plentiful early pollen (which the flowers droop to protect in wet weather) is welcomed by beetles and by a multitude of fly and bee species. Small mammals also exploit this source of protein at a time when other foods may be scarce.

OPPOSITE Bird and Anemone, *printed cotton,1881. This design, produced as a wallpaper and a chintz, evokes spring with its woodland flowers and birds. By 1877 Morris was perfecting his own technique in drawing birds (Philip Webb had drawn the birds in earlier designs).*

RIGHT Anemone nemorosa

ANTHEMIS ARVENSIS ❦ CORN CHAMOMILE (ASTERACEAE)

LEFT Anthemis arvensis (*with* Papaver rhoeas – *see page 134*)

MORRIS USED THIS small, aromatic flower in one of his many tile designs. Not as well known as the related, but introduced, common chamomile used to make teas and lawns, corn chamomile is a native annual of rough, waste and arable land, growing well on calcareous soils. It produces white, fragrant, daisy-like flowers with yellow centres from mid- to late summer and has slightly scented leaves. Now infrequently found, it is often confused with scentless mayweed.

A good source of summer nectar, this little plant may be raised each year from seed. It can grow to a height of 45cm (18in), and looks attractive in crevices and in paving, in clumps at the front of a herbaceous border or in a window box.

AQUILEGIA VULGARIS ❦ COLUMBINE (RANUNCULACEAE)

A MEMBER OF the buttercup family, the columbine was widely used in medieval times as a healing herb, then, when it fell out of favour medicinally, it continued to be cultivated in gardens as a native ornamental. There are references to it in both Chaucer and Shakespeare. With its nodding blossoms dangling from a thin stem, columbine was used by Morris in many designs, including *Daisy* wallpaper and *Bluebell* printed cotton.

This biennial or short-lived perennial was so popular in Victorian times that to Morris's chagrin plant breeders created cultivars with larger blooms. In his lectures he tried to persuade gardeners to choose the old columbine 'where the clustering doves are unmistakable and distinct, not the double one, where they run into tatters'.

Over the centuries many hybrids have been developed, including doubles of various colours, some of which have no nectar. Although now seldom seen as a wild plant in the countryside, it is still easy to buy the simple, single form.

The true columbine has purplish-blue petals and flowers in late spring and early summer. Columbine flowers more prolifically in full sun and can attain its usual height of around 60cm (24in) in one growing season. The flowering stems of some specimens reach over 1m (3ft) in some instances, although the basal leaves tend to stay in a tight clump of about 40 x 38cm (15 x 15in) or less. Easy to grow from seed sown in late spring or early summer, it can also be propagated by lifting and separating in spring or autumn. If left in a herbaceous border the plants self-seed and are an easy addition to most gardens, especially as they flower in even the shadiest corners.

The spurs contain deep-seated nectar, too difficult for butterflies to reach, but excellent for bumblebees.

LEFT Aquilegia vulgaris

OPPOSITE Daisy, *wallpaper, 1864. Columbines, seen coloured red, in profile, face up and as seedheads, as well as daisies and campion make up this design which was in production, together with* Trellis *and* Fruit *(or* Pomegranate*), in the early years of the Firm. It was inspired by an illustration in a fourteenth-century manuscript by Jean Froissart, a French historian and poet, which Morris found in the British Museum. Morris himself tried to print the plates in the company's premises at Red Lion Square.*

BELLIS PERENNIS ⁊ DAISY
LEUCANTHEMUM VULGARE ⁊ OXEYE DAISY (ASTERACEAE)

RIGHT Bellis perennis

OPPOSITE Daisy, *wallhanging, 1860. Made for the bedroom at the Red House, this features one of Morris's favourite motifs, used on wallpaper, printed cotton and tiles. Discovering a length of indigo serge in a London shop, Jane took the fabric home to Morris who was 'delighted with it and set to work at once designing flowers. These we worked in bright colour in a rough simple way.'*

BELOW One of the Daisy tiles, 1862. Daisy *proved a popular pattern and versions were also produced in the 1880s by the Dutch tile companies.*

PERENNIAL DAISIES ARE ubiquitous throughout Europe and were used by Morris in many of his designs, such as *Evenlode* and *Daisy*. England has two common white daisies: the miniature daisy, with its pink-tinged petals, abundant wherever there is short grassland or lawns, and the larger oxeye daisy, with its white ray petals and golden yellow discs, borne on tall erect stems in the summer months.

The lawn daisy, *Bellis perennis*, spreads freely in mown lawns and gardeners often remove it by the use of selective weedkillers; however, for many people it is one of summer's delights. If kept low by mowing, the tightly matted plant can form easily managed clumps up to 30–45cm (12–18in) in diameter. The flowers, borne on short 5–10cm (2–4in) hairy stalks, provide a constant source of nectar for foraging insects. Daisies thrive in a sunny spot on any moderately fertile, well-drained soil. They will grow from seed, or plants may be divided in early summer. The large-flowered double daisy, grown as a spring bedding plant, often with deep pink petals, hybridizes readily with the lawn daisy to produce curiously mixed seedlings.

The oxeye daisy, *Leucanthemum vulgare*, is a much loved wildflower often found in grassy places. Easy to grow, it is sometimes confused with its various relations. A tall, to 75cm (30in) hardy perennial, with fresh white flowers – each one wider than a thumb's breadth across – it blooms freely in midsummer. A daisy flower is actually a head of small flowers or florets. The numerous white petals are each part of a

separate floret and what appears to be a yellow disc is a mass of tightly packed tubular florets. Although largely ousted from its natural grassland habitat by modern agricultural practices, the oxeye daisy is a quick colonizer and now appears on unsprayed roadsides and railway banks, and in churchyards and gardens, particularly on light soils. It is an excellent addition to any herbaceous border, or when naturalized in a flowery meadow planting. The clumps grow large, 60cm (24in) in diameter, and they can be propagated by division in mid- or late spring. The oxeye daisy is also easily grown from seed.

The lengthy flowering season of both daisies and particularly the lawn daisy makes them a valuable source of nectar and pollen for short-tongued insects of many kinds; certain parasitic wasp species also frequent them in order to find their prey. Ants seek the fruits of the lawn daisy because of their high oil content whilst the dried seedheads of oxeye daisy are a good food source in autumn for birds.

LEFT Leucanthemum vulgare

BETULA PENDULA & SILVER BIRCH (BETULACEAE)

SLENDER AND ELEGANT, with its familiar silvery bark, birch is the most graceful of trees and a charming garden specimen, growing rapidly on most light soils. An excellent yellow-producing dye plant, it grew abundantly around Morris's factory at Merton. It appears as scrolls of foliage in the background of some of Morris's patterns.

Birch demands sun and a free-draining site. It bursts into leaf in mid-spring and the flowers appear soon afterwards, the male catkins having developed the previous autumn. Propagation is entirely by seed, which, given adequate moisture, germinates freely in light conditions. Seedlings are

LEFT Betula pendula *in flower*

readily transplanted and grown on. In ideal situations, it gains height quickly – about a metre (3ft) a year. It takes about 20 years to reach its average height of 15m (50ft), but can reach 30m (100ft) when mature at around 60 years. Slightly smaller and hardier than the silver birch, the downy birch, *Betula pubescens*, may be preferred in an upland or exposed garden.

An integral part of the food chain, birch supports a variety of caterpillars and large aphids which, in turn, provide food for predatory insects, while insectivores gorge themselves on these visiting insects. Although nectarless, birch catkins are rich in pollen, which is collected by bees. In autumn, the birch plays host to a veritable avian banquet, with a variety of birds feeding on the seeds, as do small mammals. Birds also benefit during the nesting season when birches can be relied upon to furnish the small and flexible twigs that are so vital for nest construction.

CALTHA PALUSTRIS ❧ MARSH-MARIGOLD (RANUNCULACEAE)

THIS PERENNIAL, with its heart-shaped leaves and glossy, golden-yellow flowers up to 5cm (2in) across, is, without doubt, the most handsome of the buttercup family. It was a dominant plant in the wetlands of Essex, where Morris roamed so often as a child. In a prose romance published in the *Oxford and Cambridge Magazine*, he wrote:

> I noticed every turn of the banks of the little brook, every line of the broad-leaved water flowers; I went down towards the brook, and, stooping down, gathered a knot of lush marsh-marigolds . . .

One of the first wetland plants to flower in spring, the marsh-marigold is found around rivers and wet woodland, but like many bog plants that grow naturally near water, it also grows on drier sites if planted in the shade. Plant height varies: some forms keep low, 15–23cm (6–9in), while others can reach around 45cm (18in). The profusion of flowers may be short-lived, but the luxurious dark, green leaves are attractive throughout the summer.

The marsh-marigold can be propagated by dividing clumps immediately after flowering, or by sowing seeds either in their permanent position or in a tray in early spring or autumn. Seeds need to be kept moist and shaded until they germinate. When growing on, stand the seedling pots in saucers or trays of shallow water to ensure a constantly moist soil.

The plant derives its other common name of kingcup from its large, cup-like flower, seen when the buds start to swell and open, exposing a dense cluster of anthers covered in yellow pollen. This pollen is devoured by beetles and bees.

RIGHT Caltha palustris

CARPINUS BETULUS ❧ HORNBEAM (BETULACEAE)

MORRIS SPENT HIS boyhood exploring Epping Forest on the edge of London, where he grew to know and love the hornbeams, describing them as 'interesting or romantic'. Years later, he staged a campaign to stop them being felled:

> The special character of Epping Forest was derived from the fact that by far the greater part was a wood of pollarded hornbeams . . . And I submit that no treatment of it can be tolerable which does not leave this hornbeam wood intact.

Hornbeam is often confused with beech. It has fruiting catkins and saw-toothed leaves that are slightly more matt in appearance than beech and, in areas where there are late spring frosts, it is a more satisfactory plant. Hornbeam is usually found in the coppiced understorey in oak and ash woods but, on good damp soil, it can reach a height of 15–25m (50–80ft), and sometimes over 30m (100ft). Old hornbeam coppices can be seen in many woods around London, but fully grown trees are rare.

Its close growth makes it a useful hedging plant, and it is easily coppiced (an ancient practice where stems are pruned back to the base to encourage vigorous new shoots). It thrives on heavy clay, but grows well on any good soil – other than the most acid. With its fluted trunk, smooth grey bark and attractive autumn foliage, it would be a welcome addition to any garden. Propagation of the hornbeam is by seed.

Hornbeam is host to a great number of invertebrates: the leaves and flowers are used by a range of insects including moth caterpillars, aphids and beetles.

Illustrated on page 97

107

CENTAUREA SCABIOSA & GREATER KNAPWEED (ASTERACEAE)

THIS FLOWER, which used to be found in cornfields and field borders, by hedges and on chalk downs, was used by Morris in his design for *Snakeshead* printed cotton and it is prominent in the decorative borders of his poetry books. A tall, 45–60cm (18–24in) perennial, it was a favourite in nineteenth-century cottage gardens. With attractive deeply lobed alternate leaves and reddish-purple flowers which bloom from midsummer to early autumn, greater knapweed is still a welcome addition to many gardens. It is one of a large genus of nearly 600 species of annual, biennial and perennial herbaceous plants.

Knapweed will often self-seed in a cultivated flower bed. It can also be propagated by division in the spring or by gathering seed in late summer. The seed can be kept to sow in spring, growing on the seedlings in a garden bed; or it can be sown soon after collection, keeping seedlings in pots in a cool greenhouse or cold frame through the winter.

Seedlings can be quite variable, each plant showing slight differences, notably in flower size. Although nectar is secreted deep at the base of the slender corolla tube, it rises to become easily accessible to insect visitors such as butterflies, bees and various flies. The dried, ripe seeds provide winter food for small birds.

RIGHT Centaurea scabiosa

OPPOSITE *Detail from 'Love Fulfilled', a poem from* A Book of Verse, *1870, written and 'illuminated' as a gift for Georgiana Burne-Jones. As well as knapweed, Morris included irises, larkspur, roses, tulips and martagon lilies in his delicate design.*

HAST thou longed through weary days
For the sight of one loved face,
Hast thou cried aloud for rest,
Mid the pain of sundering hours,
Cried aloud for sleep and death
Since the sweet unhoped for best
Was a shadow and a breath —
O, long now, for no fear lowers
O'er these faint feet-kissing flowers
O, rest now; and yet in sleep
All thy longing shalt thou keep.

Thou shalt rest, and have no fear
Of a dull awaking near,
Of a life for ever blind,
Uncontent and waste and wide.
Thou shalt wake, and think it sweet
That thy love is near and kind
Sweeter still for lips to meet;
Sweetest, that thine heart doth hide
Longing all unsatisfied
With all longing's answering
Howsoever close ye cling

CIRSIUM VULGARE & SPEAR THISTLE (ASTERACEAE)

BELOW LEFT Cirsium vulgare

BELOW RIGHT Thistle, *wallpaper, 1897. Always working from nature, Morris was designing wallpaper until 1895. By that time, the Morris 'house style' of plants and plant growth was so distinctive that production by Morris & Co. continued seamlessly after his death, the old patterns alongside the new. This one by John Henry Dearle is similar in style to Morris's* Oak *design (see page 139).*

WHEN MORRIS USED the stately thistle in his fabric *Rose and Thistle* – a combination first made famous by the marriage in 1503 of Henry VII's daughter Margaret Tudor to James IV of Scotland – he united the plant symbols of England and Scotland. The thistle also gives its name to a design for wallpaper.

Growing to 1.5m (5ft), the erect stems of the spear thistle and its impressive flower-heads, made up of innumerable tiny florets crowded together, make a dramatic statement in a border. The flower is also popular when dried. Spear thistle is a noxious farmland weed, so it must be grown with caution. It floats its seeds on the wind, so is widespread on waste ground, waysides and in fields. Seed germinates easily, even in dense lawns. As with many freely seeding plants, it pays to reduce excessive regeneration by cutting off the seedheads before the seeds are dispersed and using them for the bird table. Left on the plant, the seeds also provide another food source for birds who prey on the insects which live on thistles.

CORYLUS AVELLANA & HAZEL (BETULACEAE)

ONE OF THE MOST charming small trees, growing 6–12m (20–40ft) high and of immense value to wildlife, the hazel, like the silver birch, was used by Morris as a general foliage background for many of his designs. It is one of the trees which still grow at the Red House. In Morris's story, *The Wood*, a young man is led from,

> a hazel copse, like a deep hedge, into a cleared grassy space where were great grey stones lying about, as if it had been the broken doom-ring of a forgotten folk.

Hazel is invaluable for anyone wanting to create a Morris-inspired hedge, as it is an excellent hedgerow plant, offering gardeners an opportunity to attempt the ancient, but now almost abandoned, practice of coppicing. This involves a complete pruning back of all the stems to a basal stump, encouraging new vigorous shoots. Coppicing, as well as keeping the tree manageable, allows light to reach the ground so other flowers can grow. Hazel enjoys any well-drained soil and is tolerant of a range of light conditions. It can be propagated from suckers or layers – or seed. Seeds, which need protection against rodents, can be stored in cold, moist conditions over winter or sown direct into outdoor beds. They should germinate in the warmth of spring.

Hazel offers the added attraction of edible nuts. A sweet-tasting harvest can be collected from late summer into autumn – provided small mammals do not reach them first. Early clouds of pollen in spring are good for foraging bees and insects.

RIGHT Corylus avellana

CRATAEGUS MONOGYNA & HAWTHORN (ROSACEAE)

WITH A STURDY, often twisted trunk and a mantle of fragrant white blossom, this tree symbolizes the change from spring to summer and appears in Morris's epic poem *Two Red Roses Across the Moon*. Hawthorn still grows at the Red House where Morris wrote the 'Quest of Jason', one of his most tender poems:

> In the white-flowered hawthorn brake,
> Sweet, be merry for my sake;
> Twine the flowers in my hair,
> Kiss me where I am most fair . . .

Hawthorn also grew around Morris's works at Merton and would have been prominent in the hedgerows around Kelmscott Manor. In the last scene of Morris's short novel *A Dream of John Ball*, set in the Middle Ages, 'birds twittered in the trees, and in the air the scent of apple-blossom and white hawthorn hung'.

Seldom taller than 8m (26ft), hawthorn is an excellent ornamental tree for small gardens. The leaves are delicate, light green in spring and deeply lobed. Borne in dense clusters, the flowers are bisexual and each has five sepals, five petals and many stamens. Hawthorn produces abundant seed but this does not usually germinate

ABOVE Crateagus monogyna

OPPOSITE Working drawing for Jasmine, *wallpaper, c. 1872. Although the hawthorn foliage and its pink-tinged clusters of flowers are clearly seen here, in the finished wallpaper – which was printed in muted tones of green and off-white – they take a background role, and the curling tendrils of jasmine are more prominent.*

until the second spring after ripening. When mature plants are in the neighbourhood, seedlings may also appear naturally in beds and borders – a gift from birds.

Historically one of the most important of hedge plants, hawthorn is still recommended as the main component of rural hedges. It creates a dense, luxuriant living fence, its thorny stems and branches effectively repelling both burglars and cattle. It earned its old common name 'quick' during the eighteenth century because it was used as a quick-growing, stock-proof hedge. Whether grown as a hedge or tree, it is tough and stands up to extremes of temperature, winds and pollution. It seems to survive anywhere, flourishing on a variety of soils, although good drainage and a loamy soil with moderate moisture around roots will help it prosper.

Host to a variety of birds, small mammals and many species of insects, the bark, the leaves, the fruits and the dense branch structure of hawthorn combine to make it ecologically important. The nectar flow is unreliable and highly changeable – sometimes it has a sizeable amount, about once a decade! Birds use the tangle of thorns to make good nesting sites and they eat the fruits – called haws – which begin to form during late summer. Inside the fleshy edible coat, there is usually a nutlet, which becomes winter food for many birds. Small mammals also appreciate the berries.

CYTISUS SCOPARIUS & BROOM (LEGUMINOSAE)

THIS IS ONE OF THE many common plants which Morris relied on to produce a greenish-yellow for his dye vats. With its long-lasting golden-yellow flowers, borne abundantly from late spring to early summer, broom is a cheerful and familiar deciduous shrub of woodland margins, heaths and coastal regions.

Broom does not spread as rapidly as some other shrubs and it grows to about 2m (7ft) high, making it ideal for the smaller garden. However, it is relatively short-lived and looks its best when young. It enjoys a position in full sun on a light, well-drained soil and can tolerate windy conditions. The seeds can be collected from the numerous pods before they split, which they do with an audible crack on warm summer days. The plant may be propagated by cuttings in late summer.

Although broom gives no nectar, the flowers are popular with bees, which trigger an explosive pollen dispersal mechanism. The plant supports the caterpillars of many moth species, while small mammals and birds find cover and nesting sites among the dense twiggy growth.

RIGHT Cytisus scoparius

DAPHNE LAUREOLA & SPURGE LAUREL (THYMELAEACEAE)

SPURGE LAUREL WAS one of the main plants featured in a panel embroidered by May Morris in 1895. May would have drawn this either from a plant in the garden at Kelmscott Manor or at Kelmscott House. As it is one of Britain's few native evergreen shrubs – and, at not much more than 1m (3ft) high, one of the smallest – this dwarf, shrubby plant, with polished green leaves, was frequently grown in Victorian gardens. It is now quite rare in the wild.

The pale, yellow-green, slightly fragrant flowers with radiating lobes are borne in clusters from mid-winter to spring. Like its better-known cousin, *Daphne mezereon*, this shrub is a welcome addition to any garden, given the right conditions. Its early flowering period and striking black fruits make it a superb ornamental plant. Although it tolerates both sun and shade (in woodland it grows right up against the trunks of trees), it grows best in a sunny spot on a calcareous soil.

Spurge laurel can be propagated by taking heeled cuttings in summer, using a free-draining gritty compost. Germination from seed can be erratic.

The flowers are visited by pollinating moths and bumblebees for the nectar and pollen, which are especially valuable so early in the year. Although toxic to humans, its black berries are relished by a variety of birds.

RIGHT Daphne laureola

DIANTHUS DELTOIDES & MAIDEN PINK (CARYOPHYLLACEAE)

FAR LEFT Pink and Hawthorn, *tiles, designed by Morris or possibly by William De Morgan, 1887. The exaggerated petals of the prominent dianthus suggest that a garden variety was used as the source. This is another example of a design being called after a flower that takes a subsidiary role.*

LEFT Dianthus deltoides

BELOW Pink and Poppy, *design for wallpaper, c. 1880. Characteristic of Morris's work is the combination of strongly growing sinuous stems and loose-petalled flowers. Garden pinks and their relatives, border carnations, were favourites of Victorian gardeners.*

THIS LOOSELY TUFTED perennial with grass-like leaves is found on dry banks and hill pastures and was probably used by Morris in his design *Cherwell*. Its common name derives from its colour, said to be similar to a maiden's blush. As one of around 300 species in the genus *Dianthus*, maiden pink is related both to sweet williams and to the larger, more showy and more frequently seen garden pinks. It flowers in midsummer, but lacks the scent usually associated with its relatives.

Trailing or prostrate in habit, maiden pink has flowering shoots up to 45cm (18in) in height, making it suitable for rock gardens or raised beds. It can be propagated from seed or from cuttings taken immediately after flowering and inserted in pure sand until roots form.

Only butterflies and other insects possessing a long proboscis can reach the nectar hidden at the base of the stamens, as the tough calyx prevents theft 'through the back door' by biting insects.

FAGUS SYLVATICA & BEECH (FAGACEAE)

ABOVE Fagus sylvatica *in autumn*

ONE OF THE MOST impressive larger trees, beech is still as popular today as it was when Morris was alive. He wrote about it in *News from Nowhere*. The beech is a hardy native of woodlands and scrub and, contrary to common opinion, is not confined to chalk or limestone, although it has a preference for well-drained soils in full sun. As its broad-leafed canopy provides deep shade in summer, only early spring flowers are generally found growing beneath this majestic tree. Beech can reach 30m (100ft), which makes it suitable only for large gardens, but it can be an excellent hedging plant if regularly clipped, when it will keep its bronze dead leaves throughout much of the winter. It is easily propagated by sowing the nuts and then transplanting seedlings after two years.

Male and female flowers are separate but borne on the same tree in spring and early summer and are succeeded in most years by the characteristic nuts (known as mast) within their prickly husks. Being wind-pollinated, the flowers are relatively unattractive to insects, but in the autumn the nuts provide sustenance to innumerable birds and mammals.

117

FILIPENDULA ULMARIA &c MEADOWSWEET (ROSACEAE)

A TALL, FLOWERING PERENNIAL of moist woodlands, meadows and ditches, meadowsweet is one of the many plants Morris wrote about in his descriptions of the countryside he loved. The dress of flowers worn by the heroine in his fairytale from the 1890s, *The Wood Beyond the World*, contains meadowsweet, woodbine, lilies, eyebright, eglantine and mouse-ear. Botanically it was once classified as *Spiraea*, and as such gave its name to aspirin. Salicylic acid, from which a- 'spir' -in was derived, was first made from this plant in 1835, and it is still used by herbalists, in infusion, to treat headache, rheumatism and arthritis.

Meadowsweet has upright, 1.2m (4ft) stems, which hold their sizeable clusters of delicate white flowers like cotton dusters, high above the grass. Its large leaves are green above, but hairy and white below. It is called 'sweet' after its smell; not only are the flowers scented, but the leaves have such an attractive fragrance when crushed that they were strewn in medieval houses to hide unpleasant odours.

Suiting moist, loamy soil, meadowsweet prefers a position in full sun or partial shade. It can be naturalized in long grass areas, but is best established by planting large clumps. Propagation is by seed in autumn (the seed naturally germinates on bare moist soil) or by division in spring.

Because it produces an abundance of pollen, meadowsweet attracts short-tongued insects.

LEFT Filipendula ulmaria

FRAGARIA VESCA & WILD STRAWBERRY (ROSACEAE)

As both the wild and cultivated strawberry grew in Morris's gardens, it is difficult to determine which one was the inspiration for his *Strawberry Thief* textile design. The wild strawberry still grows in the kitchen courtyard at Kelmscott Manor.

A decorative, low-growing perennial with long arching runners, the wild strawberry has delicate white flowers carried in upright clusters of one to four, on short stalks above bright green leaves. If given space and sunshine the runners will spread rapidly.

The strawberry enjoys full sun on well-drained alkaline soil. With a maximum height of around 30cm (12in), it is useful as ground cover and attractive in raised beds or containers, where the runners can trail and the bright fruits be enjoyed. Easily propagated by either splitting the main clump and replanting the divisions, or more simply by the removal of the young plants produced by runners, the wild strawberry can also be sown from seed in a permanent position in early autumn.

Many insect species are known to visit the wild strawberry, especially flies and bees. The flower buds are relished by weevils and the nectar, which is secreted in a thin layer over the flower, is avidly scavenged. Ripe fruits attract birds and small mammals.

RIGHT Fragaria vesca

OVERLEAF Strawberry Thief, *printed cotton, 1883. May Morris remembered her father telling the gardener not to touch the thrushes at work on the fruit-beds, even if it meant there were fewer strawberries to eat.*

FRITILLARIA MELEAGRIS & SNAKESHEAD FRITILLARY (LILIACEAE)

ABOVE Fritillaria meleagris

RIGHT Design for Evenlode, *fabric, 1883. Morris combined past influences with glowing nature – as he so often did – in this design, named after a tributary of the Thames. Although the fritillaries, sunflowers, garden pinks and roses were everyday garden plants, the pattern was inspired by a seventeenth-century Italian brocaded velvet that the South Kensington Museum had acquired earlier that year.*

SNAKESHEAD FRITILLARY, which flowers from mid- to late spring, was a favourite motif of the Morris and the Pre-Raphaelite painters. The drooping, bell-like, red-purple to cream flowers, with their chequered shading, are prominent in at least four of Morris's designs: *Snakeshead* printed cotton, *Honeysuckle* printed cotton, *Evenlode* fabric and *Blackthorn* printed cotton. In his later novel, *The Well at the World's End* (1896), he wrote of 'the fritillary nodding at our brook's mouth . . . the willow-boughs waving on Green Eyot'.

Like many of the plants that Morris used in his designs, prose and poetry, the fritillary is found naturally in water meadows. Old fritillary meadows in the valleys of the Thames and its tributaries, around which Morris lived all his life, have since suffered the consequences of picking, uprooting, land-draining and the expansion of towns. In Morris's day, this delightful sun-loving plant was still common, especially around Walthamstow where he lived as a child. Now it is often cultivated in gardens.

The fritillary naturalizes in grass on most soils, except for dry light soils. The variably coloured flowers appear on stems 15cm (6in) long, which, in favourable situations, can increase up to 45cm (18in). They should not be cut down until the leaves have died away.

Propagation is from bulbs which should be dug up and separated in late summer when the plants die down, and then planted as soon as possible in soil that does not dry out. Each bulb needs to be planted at least 10cm (4in) deep, to avoid depredation by mice. If bulbs have been poorly stored they dry up and never produce new shoots. The plants can also be grown in cold frames from seed collected in midsummer, but it takes two years before seedlings can be planted out and then another three or four years before a bloom is seen.

It is fascinating to watch bumblebees fertilize snakeshead fritillaries, as they climb deep into the flower to reach the nectaries low on the inner surface. But many modern cultivars of this popular flower contain little or no nectar and are useless for wildlife.

GEUM RIVALE ⁊ WATER AVENS (ROSACEAE)

RIGHT Blackthorn, *wallpaper, 1892. Among flowers of hedgerow, wood and meadow in the intricate* Blackthorn *design (see page 122) is the nodding head of the now rare water avens, evident in close up. From boyhood days exploring Essex to his final years by the Thames in Oxfordshire and London, Morris loved water plants.*

BELOW Geum rivale

WHILE MANY OF THE other plants of this genus, such as the yellow-petalled wood avens, are common in hedge banks and shady gardens, water avens itself is now rare (in London it is found only in a pond in Epping Forest). In Morris's time, though, it was commonly seen and it features distinctly in his popular *Blackthorn* design.

With its creamy-pink to pinkish-purple petals, this hardy perennial brightens a damp and shady herbaceous border or a pond edge, blooming throughout summer. As the flowers tend to stand high above the leaf rosettes, it can be a useful ground cover and, when it is naturalized in grass, the dark, crimson seedheads seem to glow above the sward in the summer months. In gardens it tolerates much drier situations than when it grows wild.

The fruits are long-beaked and hooked, like those of wood avens, for dispersal by animals. Sometimes the two species cross-pollinate to produce a natural hybrid, although the petals of water avens are twice the size of those of wood avens. Both species can be propagated by sowing in a cold frame in early spring. When they are large enough to handle, they can be pricked out either into trays or individually into small pots to grow on.

The flowers attract honey- and bumble-bees; moth caterpillars feed on the leaves.

HEDERA HELIX &c IVY (ARALIACEAE)

M ORRIS GREW IVY on the walls of the Red House and it was in the garden at Kelmscott Manor, where it was immortalized by Rossetti in *Proserpine*, his portrait of Jane Morris.

Ivy is so widespread and hardy that it will grow almost anywhere, in town or country, especially in shady areas where little else will grow. It can reach up to 25m (80ft). Although its stems produce adventitious roots by which it climbs over walls, woodwork and tree trunks, ivy does not 'strangle' trees. It is not a parasite and a healthy tree will not be harmed by an evergreen cloak of ivy, as long as the crown is not covered. Ivy only affects brick or stone walls if the mortar is already loose or in otherwise bad condition. The leathery, shiny leaves are made to withstand winter conditions and the shape varies in its lobed outline, depending on the plant's age and its position.

Ivy can easily be propagated from cuttings of the juvenile growth taken in late summer. Seed can also be used but, in most gardens, seedlings will arise naturally and, if just a few plants are needed, then these can be transplanted to the intended site.

Once ivy has gained height and thickness, it is one of the most hospitable plants for wildlife, hosting a late feast for insects and birds. It has great value not only as a food source and breeding ground for native fauna but, when growing densely on trees, it also provides cosy, dry sleeping places for birds in winter.

The globe-shaped flower clusters are a superb source of late nectar for foraging insects of all kinds during the day, and moths by night. Both the ivy berries and the extensive insect population attract predatory birds and small mammals.

ABOVE Hedera helix

LEFT This sensuous portrait by Rossetti of Jane Morris as Proserpine, *1877, dominated the dining room at Kelmscott House. W.B. Yeats, a frequent visitor at Morris's Sunday night suppers, described sitting 'round a long unpolished and unpainted trestle table of new wood' beneath this painting. Other guests who dined here included George Bernard Shaw and Karl Marx's daughter, Eleanor. In the background of the picture, ivy is shown growing up the walls, just as it climbed up the walls of all Morris's houses.*

123

HYACINTHOIDES NON-SCRIPTA & BLUEBELL
(LILIACEAE SUBFAM. SCILLOIDEAE)

BLUEBELLS, WHICH STILL GROW at the Red House, were used by Morris in his cotton fabric design *Bluebell*. Brilliant carpets of these delicate, pendulous flowers in deciduous woods are one of the most spectacular sights of spring.

The one-sided and slightly drooping flower stems are characteristic of the English species, rather than the more upright and vigorous Spanish bluebell, which now sadly often replaces it in gardens. The English bluebell is smaller than its continental cousin, and is a more intense colour. It occasionally occurs in pink or white.

The bluebell is suited to naturalization in wooded areas of gardens, but it can also add early colour to herbaceous borders. Like many spring-flowering bulbs, it completes most of its growth cycle before trees and shrubs come into full leaf, and is, therefore, good for underplanting. Bulbs grown from seed take several years to mature, but the bluebell can be propagated by dividing bulbs in summer, after it has gone to rest. The leafy spring shoots tend to flatten out quite quickly, leaving the 23–38cm (9–15in) flower spikes standing free as a blue haze above the dark green leaves. The bluebell's requirements reflect its natural woodland habitat: a moist, loamy soil and some shade. It can also tolerate full sun, but, grown in this position, its colour will be less vibrant.

The bluebell, an important source of both nectar and pollen, is especially favoured by bumblebees, although various butterflies, moths, honeybees and flies also visit. Smaller insects may live in the bells and moth larvae of several species feed on the leaves. Mammals can eat the bulbs if food is scarce.

ABOVE Hyacinthoides non-scripta *growing in the garden of the Red House.*

RIGHT Drawing for Bluebell *design, 1876. Derived from a fifteenth-century printed linen at the South Kensington Museum, this shows the framework of interlacing curving lines that form the repeating pattern. The sprays of bluebells and the columbine are pink – as they appear in the finished printed cotton.*

ILEX AQUIFOLIUM ᛰ HOLLY (AQUIFOLIACEAE)

HOLLY WAS A CHILDHOOD favourite of Morris's – he admired the dark holly thickets among the hornbeams at Epping Forest and it grew in the garden at the Water House and, of course, at Kelmscott Manor. The distinctive holly leaf shape can be seen in the background of tapestries made by the Firm, and as decoration in Morris's manuscripts.

A versatile and attractive evergreen, holly favours well-drained woodlands, especially among oaks and in hedgerows. Small fragrant flowers appear in late spring and early summer, males and females being borne on different trees. The scarlet berries that brighten winter woods and gardens appear only on female plants. The prickly foliage gives way to smooth-edged leaves as the plant matures, and the silvery bark contrasts with the deep green foliage.

Although a splendid slow-growing ornamental tree – with some specimens eventually reaching 25m (80ft) – holly can also be used for hedging and windbreaks. Seeds are slow to germinate, most taking two years, so cuttings are a more reliable method of propagation.

The impenetrable nature of its foliage makes holly an excellent refuge for small birds, which also avail themselves of the berries in winter. The flowers are fragrant and attract mainly bees.

ABOVE Ilex aquifolium

IRIS FOETIDISSIMA & STINKING IRIS
IRIS PSEUDACORUS & YELLOW IRIS OR FLAG (IRIDACEAE)

ABOVE Iris foetidissima

STINKING IRIS, *Iris foetidissima*, is a flower as delicate as its name is ugly and was one of the old-fashioned flowers grown at Morris's Merton Abbey garden. Yellow flag iris, *I. pseudacorus*, the yellow iris of river banks, is one of the loveliest of spring flowers, the fleur-de-lis of legend, used by Morris in his design for the printed cotton *Iris* of 1876.

The common name 'stinking iris' relates to the smell emitted when the lustrous long leaves are crushed. To some, the odour is more like roast beef, hence its alternative name, 'roast beef plant'. The flowers are not outstanding, but the abundant narrow leaves stay green all winter, and the orange-red seeds are spectacular as winter display.

Preferring chalky soil, stinking iris is found in woods and hedges, and on banks and cliffs. Its distinctive purplish flowers are delicately marked with darker, greyish-purple veins and appear from late spring to midsummer. The three sepals and three petals all look like petals and are known as 'tepals'. Stinking iris is a versatile, valuable garden plant, easy to grow even in dry areas and tolerant of some shade. It provides handsome foliage and colour in summer as well as late season interest.

Yellow flag iris is an upright perennial of river banks, pond margins and marshland. Its sword-like leaves are one of the hallmarks of wetlands from early to midsummer. With its upright, 1.5m (5ft) flower spikes, impressive flowers and striking foliage, it makes a superb plant for water gardens and pond margins, but does equally well in much drier conditions and is popular in herbaceous borders. It likes moisture and full sun, but will tolerate light shade. If left for a few years, this iris grows into large clumps – up to 1.2m (4ft) high and 2m (7ft)

or more across. It is best repropagated by division of the rhizomes in late summer, about every three years, but alternatively seeds can be sown in autumn. The seeds float on water, germinating the following summer if they land on a bare patch of mud.

Yellow iris is an excellent plant for wildlife – it provides nectar and pollen and also, in watery situations, offers shelter to amphibians and other aquatic creatures among its stems. Predominantly pollinated by bees, but other aerial insects also visit.

ABOVE Iris pseudacorus

RIGHT Iris, *wallpaper, designed by John Henry Dearle in* c. 1887. *By the beginning of 1887 Morris was so deeply involved in his political activities and lectures that he increasingly delegated work to Dearle, who continued to produce work long after Morris's death.*

LONICERA PERICLYMENUM ⚭ HONEYSUCKLE
(CAPRIFOLIACEAE)

OPPOSITE Honeysuckle, *wallpaper, 1883. This shows how closely Morris observed his subject matter.*

BELOW *Design for* Honeysuckle, *1876. The enduring popularity of this fabric is a tribute to Morris's extraordinary ability to handle a highly complex design in which he brought together crown imperials, fritillaries and yew twigs as well as honeysuckle.*

MORRIS USED HONEYSUCKLE in several designs, including one of his best-selling fabrics, *Honeysuckle* (see page 148). The distinctive flowers of honeysuckle, with their long style projecting beyond the funnel-like tube, were also used in the *Honeysuckle* wallpaper designs, and the tapestry *Woodpecker*.

Honeysuckle is a versatile and easy addition to all gardens. Groups of flowers, each one small with five sepals, start appearing in early summer and continue until autumn. A familiar sight clambering through hedges and on trellises, walls and other trees and shrubs, it climbs by twining its long reddish-purple, woody stems in a clockwise direction around the stems of stronger supporting plants. Honeysuckle can be vigorous, even invasive, and climbs 6–10m (20–33ft), where there is no competition. If left in dense clumps, it makes a good nesting site for birds. As well as climbing upwards honeysuckle can be grown as ground cover. It can be raised from late summer cuttings, and planted out after twelve months in clusters of two or three.

Honeysuckle is a flower of the night: its many trumpet-shaped blooms only give off their pervasive scent as they fill with nectar in the evening. Having a long tube to the corolla, the flower is adapted to entice night-visiting moths – the only insects with a proboscis long enough to penetrate it. On warm calm evenings moth visits are so frequent that the next morning the flowers are transformed – fertilized flowers change from white to yellow, and the pollen is entirely removed.

LYTHRUM SALICARIA & PURPLE LOOSESTRIFE
(LYTHRACEAE)

ONE OF THE WATERSIDE plants loved by Morris, purple loosestrife was immortalized by the Pre-Raphaelite artist, John Everett Millais, in *Ophelia*, painted in 1851 on the Hogsmill river in Surrey, a tributary of the Thames.

Tough and tall, this ornamental perennial can be used effectively in borders, as a pond marginal or naturalized in wet grassland. Growing up to 1.2m (4ft), or even 2m (7ft) on a good site, it has candle-like, purple-flower-covered spikes from mid- to late summer. As with many 'simple plants', in some situations it can become invasive. (Indeed, it has become so invasive in North America – and in the process has destroyed large areas of valuable wetlands – that strenuous efforts are now being made to eradicate it.) To keep it in check, the flowering spikes should be cut back before the seeds have formed. It can also be divided and some of the plant discarded if it has outgrown its allotted space.

After flowering, the stems become woody, lasting as dead canes for two or more years. They may either be cut down in winter, or just shortened back to provide supports for the new season's growth. It self-seeds prolifically, but since the resultant seedlings do not transplant easily, it may be easier to propagate by sowing seeds in a cold frame in spring, pricking them out when they are large enough, and planting ready for the summer.

The nectar and pollen are sought after by small-tongued bees, while butterflies seek the nectar.

ABOVE Lythrum salicaria

LEFT Ophelia *by Millais, 1851. 'Truth to Nature' – the aspect of Pre-Raphaelite painting that so appealed to Morris – is seen here in the faithful representation of riverside flowers including purple loosestrife, wild roses, willow trees and irises.*

131

NARCISSUS PSEUDONARCISSUS *&* WILD DAFFODIL
(LILIACEAE SUBFAM. AMARYLLIDOIDEAE)

THE DAFFODIL FEATURES in a textile of the same name produced by Morris & Co. Formerly a common native of damp woodlands, the wild daffodil is now relatively rare. It is smaller and more delicate than its hybrid cultivated brethren, and appears from late winter to mid-spring, when solitary flowers form on single stems around 30cm (12in) high.

Perfect for naturalization, the daffodil grows well under native deciduous trees, but flowers and thrives better in moist grassland or at the foot of hedges where it self-seeds, as well as producing daughter bulbs. A fertile, moist but free-draining soil is best, in a sunny or partially shaded location. Seeds can be collected and sown in beds during autumn, or bulb clumps of older plants may be divided when dormant.

The early nectar and pollen of this plant are welcomed by insects at a time when relatively few other plants are in flower. It is pollinated by early flying, short-tongued bumblebees, which push past the central column of anthers surrounding the single style to reach the nectar at its base. Early-flying flies, drone-flies and other bees also visit but the large bumblebee can barely fit inside the flower. Some of these visitors will perforate the flower tube to get at the nectar, making feeding easier during subsequent visits by short-tongued insects.

OPPOSITE Daffodil, *printed cotton, designed by John Henry Dearle, c. 1891. The vibrant pattern, with its sinuous vertical stems, sprays of flowers and curling leaves, demonstrates how well Morris's teachings were absorbed by his employees.*

LEFT Narcissus pseudonarcissus

PAPAVER RHOEAS *&* COMMON POPPY
GLAUCIUM FLAVUM *&* YELLOW HORNED POPPY (PAPAVERACEAE)

POPPIES FEATURE IN Morris's famous tapestry *The Forest* for which it is likely that he used both common and yellow horned poppies as models and the common poppy appears in the *Orchard* tapestry. Morris also used the more exotic opium poppy – often depicting it from the back – in his more complex designs.

The common poppy, *Papaver rhoeas*, is one of the most well-loved summer meadow flowers, widespread in lowland fields, on hedge banks and in gardens. The papery, blood-red flowers usually last only a day, but they are borne in profusion from late spring throughout the summer. The flowers are followed by distinctive 'pepper-pot' seed pods. The poppy will enhance any garden, yet, because this hardy annual competes with cereals in fields, it is often denigrated as a weed. It grows well in sun or partial shade, even on poor soil as long as it is free-draining. The stems can reach 60cm (24in) or more. On good soil, a single seedling can quickly form a 60 x 60cm (24in x 24in) clump.

The poppy self-seeds with alacrity, but gardeners can collect seeds easily. Children often enjoy doing this: ripe heads are put upside-down into a paper bag, and the stems and the bag top are tied together to allow the seeds to dry; then they are shaken into the bottom of the bag and kept cool and dry until sowing. If seeds are sown at the end of summer, seedlings start coming through in autumn and winter and on into early spring. Seeds can live for some years in the soil, germinating when the ground is cultivated and they are exposed to light.

For germination the poppy needs bare soil, which means either sowing in an annually prepared bed or, perhaps, on clear ground around the base of shrubs or small trees. Under dense trees it becomes lank, producing few flowers. Because it seeds so freely, the poppy is best managed in its own patch of the garden.

Although the flowers lack nectar, the pollen is rich in proteins and poppies have considerable appeal for wildlife. Their vivid red acts as a beacon, and pollen-seeking bumble- and honeybees see the flower in an ultraviolet pattern. Beetles and hoverflies also seek the abundant pollen.

The yellow horned poppy, *Glaucium flavum*, is a biennial or short-lived perennial herb. A handsome sea-shore plant, anchored by a deep, stout, tap-root, it has many-branched hairless stems, up to 90cm (36in), that carry lobed lower leaves with rough-haired stalks, and stalkless upper leaves, whose bases clasp the stem. The dazzling, four-petalled, yellow flowers, up to 9cm (3½in) in diameter, eventually develop into long seed pods, themselves up to 30cm (12in) long when ripe. They then split into two equal halves from the top.

With its large flowers, amazing seed horns and attractive foliage, the yellow horned poppy is a useful plant for a dry, sunny position in a spacious herbaceous border. It is easily propagated from seed sown in a gritty compost, or by division in spring or autumn and is widely available from nurseries where an orange form, *G. flavum* f. *fulvum*, may also be offered.

Like other poppies, the yellow horned poppy is a pollen plant, attracting small solitary bees, bumblebees and beetles. Its colourful flowers serve them with copious amounts of food from a forest of stamens through which they scramble, covering themselves in pollen, which they then carry to other flowers. This is often called 'mess and spoil' pollination.

ABOVE Papaver rhoeas

OPPOSITE Embroidered bed curtain at Kelmscott Manor, 1883. W.B. Yeats's sister, Lily, worked for Morris and then for May Morris as an embroiderer. 'The hangings round Morris's big bed . . . with their verses about lying happily in bed . . . were from her needle, though not from her design,' according to Yeats.

POTENTILLA ERECTA ℰ TORMENTIL
POTENTILLA NEUMANNIANA ℰ SPRING CINQUEFOIL (ROSACEAE)

I N MORRIS'S FABRIC DESIGN *Rose*, potentillas mingle with Eastern tulips, birds and the elaborate roses. Today, countless hybrid potentillas are for sale in garden centres, many of them showy doubles, used for their summer colour.

Tormentil, *Potentilla erecta*, has four-petalled saucer-shaped yellow flowers with nectaries, situated around a central disc, frequented, like most spring nectar plants, by small bees, flies and hoverflies. This small perennial, with a basal leaf rosette and flower stems rising to 45cm (18in), grows mostly on acid soils. The flowers set an abundance of small, light seeds, which can be blown a considerable distance.

Spring cinquefoil, *Potentilla neumanniana*, a spring-flowering perennial with small, bright yellow flowers, is one of the lesser known of the 500 species of the genus *Potentilla*. The stubby new stems grow horizontally, so that the plant forms a thick mat, the flowers held on 10cm (4in) stems. A good border plant, it is easily grown in well-drained loam, and though it prefers sun it will happily endure semi-shade.

ABOVE Design for Rose, *1887. The five-petalled potentillas appear in the background of this design for a furnishing fabric.*

RIGHT Potentilla neumanniana

PRIMULA VULGARIS &c PRIMROSE (PRIMULACEAE)

THIS EVOCATIVE PLANT grew at the Red House and was used by Morris both as a watermark for paper at the Kelmscott Press and as a motif in one of his glazed tiles.

Treasured as a herald of spring, these hardy flowers with pale-coloured petals – usually yellow, but sometimes white or reddish-pink – are the first of the native primulas to bloom each year. They were made popular during Morris's lifetime by the Prime Minister, Benjamin Disraeli, Lord Beaconsfield, who was a political foe of Morris's but, like Morris, had been brought up in Walthamstow. Disraeli always wore a primrose in his buttonhole and in 1882, a year after his death, Primrose Day came into being on 19 April.

Found in damp, heavy soils in open woodlands, hedgerows and meadows, the primrose is now less common owing to urban sprawl and modern farming practices. It can be grown in most situations; in containers near the house, naturalized in semi-shaded grass areas, or used in bold clumps in borders – even in shady sites.

The primrose can be propagated by division after flowering in late spring, or by seed in early summer. The natural dispersal is by ants, which carry away the sticky seeds. The primrose increases from seed better in gardens, where there is constant slight soil disturbance and close mowing to keep grass down, than in its natural woodland habitat.

As it is one of the earliest flowers to produce nectar, this hardy plant is much sought after by a variety of insects, including long-tongued bees, long-tongued flies and butterflies. Gardeners, though, often unwittingly plant only the showy hybrids which provide no nectar. Many varieties sold in garden centres are sterile doubles with exaggerated petals and harsh colours.

ABOVE Primula vulgaris

RIGHT Primrose, *tile, 1862–5. Inspired by medieval herbals, and also influenced by traditional Dutch and English tiles, this simple design was hand painted by Morris on to a ready-glazed tile.*

137

PRUNUS SPINOSA & BLACKTHORN OR SLOE
(ROSACEAE)

RIGHT Blackthorn *wallpaper, 1892. This is one of Morris's last and most popular patterns (see page 122). The simple flowers – blackthorn blossom, fritillaries, water avens and violets – are entwined in a complex structure, emphasizing the exuberance of the simple plants which he so enjoyed in his gardens.*

BELOW Prunus spinosa

THIS DENSELY SPIKED BUSH with black shoots has the first spring blossom in countryside hedges. It grew around Morris's works at Merton, becoming the inspiration for his complex design *Blackthorn*.

Prunus spinosa is rarely large enough to be called a tree, although it can reach 4–5m (13–16¼ft) and its compact spiny form has made it a popular plant for hedges. In small gardens, due to its spreading habit and sharp thorns, it needs to be kept under control. Those who cultivate it are rewarded with crops of sloes – beautiful, small, purplish-black, plum-like fruits with a slight bloom – which are too tart to eat, but make a delicious drink when steeped in gin.

Growing on all but the most acid of soils, blackthorn is happiest on a well-drained site with lime. Although it can be propagated from seed, it suckers freely, and these can be removed and grown on.

The brilliant white, fragrant blossom is produced as the days begin to lengthen in late spring, and before the leaves appear on the branches. It is sometimes confused with hawthorn, which flowers later, after the blackthorn comes into leaf.

Blackthorn is rich in nectar and attracts a variety of insects, especially butterflies and moths, wasps and hoverflies. The list of moth and butterfly larvae that lay eggs on blackthorn is extensive. Beetles and bugs relish the densely packed fruits, as do the many birds that feed on them during autumn, and find shelter and nest sites in its impenetrable foliage.

QUERCUS ROBUR ❦ ENGLISH OR PEDUNCULATE OAK
QUERCUS PETRAEA ❦ SESSILE OAK (FAGACEAE)

RIGHT Oak, furnishing fabric, 1881. The distinctive lobed leaves of oak, which still grows at the Red House, inspired this fabric and they were later used as motifs in the background of embroideries.

BELOW Quercus robur

THE DISTINCTIVE LOBED LEAVES of the national tree of England, which still grows at the Red House, are featured in Morris's *Brother Rabbit* and *Oak* designs, and the oak is often referred to in his prose and letters. In a letter to Georgiana Burne-Jones, he wrote about visiting the De Morgans in Surrey, 'the best part [of it] the beauty of the oaks, now in their new foliage hanging about the rare cornfields . . .'

Majestic, sturdy and stately, with its rugged, greyish, brown bark, whether relatively young or over a thousand years old, oak is a tree most people are proud to own. It is a good 'mother' tree as its roots go deep, creating less competition with other plants which happily grow in its shade. Flourishing in full sun to partial shade, in almost any type of soil, but preferring neutral or lime-rich soils, it needs reasonable rainfall to become established. The oak is excellent either as a tree or hedging, deep humus forms from its fallen leaves, creating a rich growing medium. A young oak often holds on to its dead autumn leaves, providing attractive winter foliage.

Two species of oak are indigenous to the countryside of Morris's boyhood – the pedunculate oak, *Quercus robur*, which favours clay and heavy loam, and the sessile oak, *Q. petraea*, which favours sandier, shallower soils. Differences can be seen in spring when they come into bloom. The flowers and acorns of *Q. robur* are borne on stalks, in contrast to those of *Q. petraea* which are stalkless. Paradoxically, the leaves of *Q. robur* are short stalked, while those of *Q. petraea* are stalked. Both are large and long-lived trees, the latter reaching 40m (131ft) or more, and though tolerant of pruning, they are best suited to large gardens.

The oak can be raised from acorns which need to be collected soon after they fall and sown promptly in mouse-proof beds. The following spring they will germinate, producing a 6–8cm (3–4in) stem and a sturdy root by midsummer, but they are best kept in 2–3 litre (3½–5 pint) pots and not planted until their second year.

The oak is a most valuable tree for wildlife, boasting a large number of associated insect species; it plays host to lichens and fungi and attracts a variety of small mammals.

ROSA CANINA ℰ DOG-ROSE (ROSACEAE)

THE ROSE WAS ONE OF Morris's best-loved flowers: he grew them on the walls of the Red House and over the porch at Kelmscott Manor; they dominate his designs *Trellis* and *Rose and Thistle*; and they appear in his verse. The arching stems of briar roses are evident in many paintings by his lifelong friend Edward Burne-Jones. In Morris's epic poem, *The Earthly Paradise*, he describes how in 'that sweet close was trellised the bewildering rose . . .'

Wild climbing roses are excellent for informal gardens. They are tolerant of most soil types, but thrive on rich moisture-retentive loams in sunny or partially shaded situations. As they flower more freely in full sun, roses are often trained against house walls, but these can get too hot in summertime, so it is better to grow roses up trellises or frames, with a block between the support and the wall. Rambling wild roses can also be trained along chains to form a hedge, over old tree stumps, or may be left unchecked so that they can flourish as they do in the countryside – tumbling over ancient hedges and giving rural lanes colour and scent. Flowers differ in appearance, flushed with various shades of pink and white. The delicate blooms contrast with the bright green of the leaves.

The dog-rose, *Rosa canina*, bears pale pink or white flowers with yellow stamens and, later, glossy red hips. It is delightful as a garden shrub or used as a climber on trellises. It grows to 3–4m (10–13ft) and its piercing thorns make it a good anti-burglar device, if grown below and around windows. Like all prickly shrubs it makes a perfect anti-cat bush below a bird table.

The dog-rose is so robust that in the past rose growers used it to provide rootstocks on which to graft the more delicate hybrid roses. Dog-roses can be raised from seed, which must be given moist chilling over winter. Some roses will sucker, thus giving an easy means of increase, whilst the non-suckering forms can usually be increased by means of semi-ripe summer or autumn hardwood cuttings.

The vigorous dog-rose is host to many beetles. The summer flowers are also an excellent source of pollen for hoverflies, sawflies and all kinds of bees and wasps. The hips are a welcome source of winter food for birds. Although, unfortunately, roses attract aphids, these provide tasty food for nestling birds.

Other wild roses suitable for the garden are the burnet rose, *R. pimpinellifolia*, the field-rose, *R. arvensis* and the sweetbriar, *R. rubiginosa*, which grows to around 2m (6–7ft), with tiny glands beneath its leaves, which are fragrant when they are rubbed. The field-rose is smaller, 1–2m (3–7ft), than the dog-rose and, being more tolerant of shade and poor drainage, it is easier to manage in the garden.

The burnet-rose is smaller still and, with its fine pinnate leaves, ivory flowers and shiny black hips, it is an excellent garden plant. It forms a clump of up to 1m (3ft) in height and mixes well in a herbaceous border.

ABOVE Rosa canina

ABOVE Rose and Thistle, *fabric, 1882. In his design,*
Morris characteristically contrasted the stiff, dominant forms
of pomegranates, much as they are depicted in medieval textiles,
with the more natural-looking flowers of roses and thistles.

LEFT Rosa pimpinellifolia

RUBUS FRUTICOSUS AGG.
❦ BRAMBLE OR BLACKBERRY (ROSACEAE)

MORRIS SHOWED BRAMBLE in two of his tapestries, but it is not clear which species he used of this vigorous spreading woody climber. There are so many micro-species of bramble that it is difficult to tell them apart. It is unlikely that Morris grew brambles in the formal part of his garden, but they would have been growing around Kelmscott Manor.

The cultivation of the hardy bramble presents no problems and it can be grown in sunny positions in gardens with great effect, as long as it is encouraged to grow upwards and not along the ground. If the arching stems reach the ground, they root at their tips and the plant becomes truly invasive.

When trained against a wall, or high fence – or anywhere where its spreading habit and hook-like prickles do not interfere with other plants – it is attractive. It likes a loamy soil and needs support: a wall, trellis, fence or stout post, against which the main shoots can be loosely tied. On a good soil, the shoots can scramble 4–5m (13–16ft) up a tree. Propagation is by rooted stem tips or stolons. This can be allowed to happen naturally, or encouraged by pegging down shoots. Seedlings, which vary in the quality of their fruit, occur naturally, having been spread by birds – usually where not required!

The white or pink flowers can be eye-catching on a well-trained plant, and they are a useful source of pollen for bees and beetles. The main attraction, however, is the bramble's leaves and its juicy berries. At the end of summer, the freshly picked fruit is abundant and delicious for both birds and people.

ABOVE Rubus fruticosus

SALIX CAPREA ❦ GOAT OR PUSSY WILLOW
(SALICACEAE)

ABOVE The male flowers of Salix caprea

WILLOW WAS ONE OF Morris's favourite plants. Its bark, twigs and leaves traditionally produced browns, fawns and purples for the dye vat and he also used it in many of his designs, including the famous wallpaper and fabrics *Willow* and *Willow Boughs*, *Tulip and Willow* and *Scroll*. A background of willows is also found in Morris wallpapers such as *Powdered* and *Lily*. The willow in Morris's designs has been attributed to a botanical drawing in Gerard's sixteenth-century *Herball*, but in her biography of her father May Morris described how closely he looked at the willows at Kelmscott Manor:

> We were walking one day by our little stream that runs into Thames, and my Father pointed out the detail and variety in the leaf-forms, and soon afterwards this paper was done, a keenly-observed rendering of our willows that has embowered many a London living-room . . .

In Morris's book *A Dream of John Ball*, the hero laments the destruction of trees:

> On the other side of the water the few willow trees left us by the Thames Conservancy looked doubtfully alive against the bleak sky. . .

In his own life, he made pleas for the local native river flora to be preserved.

The goat or pussy willow, *Salix caprea*, with its attractive fluffy flowers, is one of the earliest willow species to come into flower, the familiar catkins appearing before the leaves. Willows have separate male and female plants, but bisexual forms occur. The male catkins are white and silky,

LEFT Willow Boughs, *wallpaper, 1887. With its strong structure of upwardly winding leafy willow boughs and its subtle colouring, this has become Morris's best-known design, used for fabric as well as wallpaper.*

143

later becoming golden-yellow, while the silvery female catkins become greenish. Forming a bush or tree, goat willow makes a charming garden plant and does not require the wet conditions typical of other willows. It can grow eventually to a height of around 10m (33ft) or more, but with regular coppicing or pollarding it can easily be kept within the bounds of a normal garden.

Willow is a remarkably hospitable tree for wildlife. Its catkins provide the first energy-giving nectar to butterflies when they emerge from hibernation in spring, as well as to early foraging bees, who also take the pollen. Many insect species can be harboured by this willow, including beetles, hoverflies and ants, making it a favourite of insectivorous birds. The caterpillars of many moths feed on the foliage.

Similar to the goat willow but slightly smaller, growing to 9m (30ft), the almond willow, *S. triandra*, is also eminently suitable for gardens, although it may prefer a wetter environment. The male catkins are fragrant, and this willow has long been cultivated for basket-making.

The possible subjects for Morris's designs, the white willow, *S. alba*, and crack willow, *S. fragilis*, were familiar streamside trees of his countryside and, though lovely in themselves, are less well suited to small gardens, since the former can reach 33m (108ft) and the latter sometimes more than 25m (80ft).

RIGHT Tulip and Willow, *furnishing fabric, c. 1875. In this design, Morris combined the natural with the formal and the present with echoes of the past.*
Willows grew by the Thames at Kelmscott Manor and The Tulip Garden *by Peter Brueghel the Younger (1564–1637) was one of his favourite paintings. It hangs in the house to this day.*

SERRATULA TINCTORIA & SAW-WORT (ASTERACEAE)

THIS ROBUST PLANT with purple-tinged bracts and pink flower heads was for centuries a source of colouring for woollen cloth. Morris used it and would have made a dye by boiling the leaves and then adding alum to produce a yellow-green colour. Both the common and the Latin names refer to the jagged edges of these productive leaves; 'serratula' is from the Latin for 'a little saw'; similarly, saw-wort refers to the tooth-like leaf margins. Once found commonly on cliff-tops, grassland, open woodland and rocky streamsides on well-drained soils, it is now seen only in isolated places. It is 200 years since it was observed at the edge of Epping Forest.

Although smaller, the saw-wort is similar in appearance to knapweed (see page 108), to which it is closely related. Like knapweed, it flowers from midsummer to early autumn. Saw-wort can be naturalized in a flowering lawn or used in a herbaceous bed, though it might need staking to prevent the flowering stems flopping over. In rich soils it can reach nearly 1m (3ft) but, in poor exposed conditions, it is only around 10cm (4in) high. For propagation details see knapweed. Nectar rises up the tube, making it easily accessible to insect visitors, such as butterflies, bees and various flies. The dried ripe seeds provide excellent winter food for small birds.

ABOVE Serratula tinctoria

SILENE DIOICA & RED CAMPION
SILENE VULGARIS & BLADDER CAMPION (CARYOPHYLLACEAE)

ABOVE Silene dioica

LIKE SO MANY PLANTS that Morris depicted in his designs, campions were common flowers of the wild spaces of London. He used campion in his design for the wallpaper *Daisy*.

These hardy perennials are common along waysides of all kinds and on rough grassland and waste ground. Campion seeds shed early, while flowering continues higher up the plant, and this helps its survival along summer-mown verges. Red campion, *Silene dioica*, can be recognized by its dark pink flowers. The slender stems of the larger campions reach nearly 1m (3ft), carrying their neat foliage and distinctly formed flowers, each with five bifid petals, which are present from mid-spring until the end of the summer. Suitable for the herbaceous border, rock gardens, grassy habitats and even window boxes, this plant is easily raised from collected seed or propagated by division in spring. Though it tolerates light soils, it is at its most prolific in moist soils and enjoys full sun.

White campion, *Silene latifolia*, is, like most white flowers, a flower of the night. The slight scent of the flowers, which is only emitted after dusk, attracts pollinating moths seeking the nectar at the bottom of the long tubular flowers.

A tall-growing plant with stalkless leaves, white campion is a short-lived perennial. Like its cousin, the bladder campion, it prefers an open sunny position and suits most soils, but not damp areas. It looks attractive in gardens when grown in small clumps. If grown near red campion, the two will hybridize, a pink form appearing the next year.

Bladder campion, *Silene vulgaris*, is a hardy perennial with thin stems above waxy grey-green foliage. It is excellent for limestone rock gardens as well as borders or grassy habitats. Its small white flowers emit a pleasant clove-like aroma. Common along waysides and on rough waste ground, it is the smallest of the three campions mentioned here, growing to around 80cm (32in). Bladder campion is related to sea campion, *S. maritima*, with which it sometimes cross-breeds. It will survive in sandy, windswept coastal areas.

The nectar in campions is located deep within the flowers so is usually available only to long-tongued insects such as butterflies and some moths. Short-tongued bees may rob the flower by cutting a hole at its base to acquire nectar without pollinating the plant.

BELOW Silene vulgaris

SOLANUM DULCAMARA ⁊ BITTERSWEET OR WOODY NIGHTSHADE
(SOLANACEAE)

IN HIS SHORT STORY 'The Story of the Unknown Church', Morris referred to this plant as deadly nightshade:

> . . . deadly nightshade, La bella donna,
> O! so beautiful; red berry, and purple,
> yellow-spiked flower, and deadly,
> cruel-looking, dark green leaf . . .

In fact the description refers to the woody nightshade, which also appears in Morris's *Acanthus and Vine* tapestry.

This little-cultivated native member of the potato family is widely distributed in low-lying situations. Its dramatic violet-blue, five-petalled flowers with distinctive yellow anthers appear in early summer and last through the season, dangling from the stems, eventually forming a red berry which is mildly poisonous. A woody, climbing, deciduous perennial with soft, semi-woody shoots, it grows quickly to 3m (10ft) or more. When it dies back in winter, only the base remains woody. Generally regarded as a weed, it has value as a garden climber if helped with a trellis or support. As it tolerates shade and dry conditions, it can be useful in shady town gardens – but it does not like damp areas or an exposed site.

Propagation is easy if soft or semi-hard cuttings are taken in summer. The stems layer and sucker naturally and these ready-rooted parts can easily be used to produce new plants. Although it was used in the past for the treatment of skin abscesses, all parts of the plant are poisonous. The unripe fruits can irritate the stomach and the intestines, and affect the central nervous system.

Gardeners should not be deterred, after all, many garden plants, including the green parts of its relative, the potato, are also toxic.

The flowers are a source of pollen for bees, but it has little or no nectar. The bees can be seen clinging to the anther cone and rapidly vibrating the anthers to release their pollen from holes at the tips.

ABOVE LEFT Acanthus and Vine, *Morris's first tapestry, 1879. The distinctive blue flowers and pointed yellow cones of woody nightshade appear on the decorative border. In contrast to these and the simple rose buds which Morris drew directly from nature, the swirling forms of the acanthus leaves were taken from books of classical ornamental design.*

ABOVE RIGHT Solanum dulcamara

147

TAXUS BACCATA & YEW
(TAXACEAE)

YEW FORMED AN IMPRESSIVE hedge in the garden at Kelmscott Manor. In the magazine, *The Quest*, in 1894, Morris described part of it:

> Going under an arch opening in the yew hedge which makes a little garth about a low door in the middle of the north wall, one comes into a curious passage or lobby . . .

In the last scene of Morris's short story *The Roots of the Mountains* (1889), he describes a tunnel of yew:

> But lo! At last at the garden's end is the yew-walk arched over for thee, and thou canst not see whereby to enter it; but I, I know it, and I lead thee into and along the dark tunnel through the moonlight . . .

Yew, with its reddish-brown bark, is a traditional feature of the English landscape, growing on chalk and limestone downs and in churchyards. It is most effective as a

LEFT Honeysuckle, *printed cotton, 1876. Yew forms the background for this, one of Morris's most successful designs. 'If the* Wandle *is literally the most "splendid" of Morris's designs, the* Honeysuckle *will seem to be the most Morrisian in character of all his pattern-making in mid-life,' said May Morris in her biography of her father. 'The crown imperial with its graceful top-knot, the great poppy whose leaves form an inner net, the honeysuckle, the fritillaries, the background of yew-twigs, all these elements, looking as if they were copied straight from the garden, are brought together in a decoration for wall or window unique in the history of design past or present.'*

garden hedge, giving a rich green backdrop that contrasts well with flowers. Yew can also be trained to make a shady arbour or a niche for statue or a seat.

As a tree it is long-lived, many venerable twisted specimens lasting for over a thousand years. As a hedge, too, it can survive for generations and there are some 300-year-old examples. Slow growing, it responds to irrigation. Equally, it is tolerant of drought. Though not a problem in a garden maker's lifetime, yew can eventually grow to a height of over 27m (90ft).

It may be propagated from seed, which can take two years or more to germinate, and this is best kept out of doors stratified in leaf mould in a cool moist place until germinated. If not protected, rodents will eat the young seedlings.

Male and female flowers appear on different trees from mid-winter until spring. The small cones in the males produce clouds of pollen – a good food supply for early flying insects such as bumblebees. Its feathery evergreen foliage provides welcome winter cover for wildlife. From late summer the deep red flesh which ripens, cup-like, around the seeds, is avidly devoured by many birds. But the seeds and all parts of yew are toxic to man and most animals.

ABOVE Taxus baccata

THYMUS POLYTRICHUS SSP. BRITANNICUS
❦ WILD THYME (LAMIACEAE)

Morris so liked thyme that he picked some in Iceland and posted it back to Kelmscott Manor to his daughters.

There are three species of thyme native to Morris's countryside, all of which are aromatic and distinguished by their creeping mat-like clumps: *Thymus polytrichus* ssp. *britannicus*, *T. pulegioides* and *T. serpyllum*. *T. polytrichus* has the advantage of being very robust and bearing rose-purple flowers throughout the summer. The garden thyme grown by most people for culinary use, *T. vulgaris*, is native to Spain and Italy.

Although best propagated by division in mid- or late spring, these aromatic plants can also be grown from seed. Once sown and established, they last for years, and keep self-seeding. Thyme relishes warm sunny sites, and grows well in cracks or prepared sites in paving, or in raised beds or large shallow containers.

The nectar-rich flowers attract moths, butterflies, bees and solitary wasps.

LEFT Thymus polytrichus *ssp.* britannicus

149

VERONICA CHAMAEDRYS &c GERMANDER SPEEDWELL
VERONICA SPICATA &c SPIKED SPEEDWELL (SCROPHULARIACEAE)

IT IS PROBABLE THAT Morris used germander speedwell, *Veronica chamaedrys*, in his *Eyebright* design, although the spiked speedwell, *V. spicata*, is another possible candidate.

Germander speedwell derives its name from the myth that it speeds travellers on their journey. With its slender, trailing stems growing up to 45cm (18in) high, and its bright blue flowers with white centres, this perennial makes an attractive border plant. Common as a wild plant in gardens in Morris's day, its place as an enjoyed garden weed has now been taken by the similar but introduced annual, field speedwell, *V. persica*, which was imported not long before Morris was born. The germander speedwell grows readily from seed.

This is a plant that appears to have been made for hoverflies, which flock to it, flying straight to the bright blue corolla – as do small bees and other insects.

Even in Morris's time, spiked speedwell, *V. spicata*, was rare in the wild, although it was a popular cottage-garden plant. In summer and early autumn, the numerous blue flowers of this impressive wild perennial, packed densely on to spikes, break into bloom. Today many gardeners grow hybrids in blue, white or pink, and also the European version, *V. longifolia*.

The flowering stems of spiked speedwell grow to about 60cm (24in), or taller at times, and are slightly woody at their base when mature. It has a compact rhizome and does not spread rapidly, but needs regular division in many soils, or propagation from spring cuttings to keep a healthy growth. A sunny border and a light soil suit it well. The tubular flowers are a good source of nectar and pollen for many insects, including bees and hoverflies. When a fly wants to settle to get to the nectar, it drags the two stamens together, and then rests upon them using the style for balance.

ABOVE LEFT Veronica spicata

ABOVE RIGHT Veronica chamaedrys

OPPOSITE Powdered, *wallpaper, 1874. Arching willow leaves form a background to this pattern which was printed first as a wallpaper and then as a chintz. The flowers depicted include speedwell and greater knapweed, both popular cottage-garden plants at the time.*

VIOLA RIVINIANA ❦ COMMON VIOLET OR DOG-VIOLET
VIOLA TRICOLOR ❦ HEARTSEASE OR WILD PANSY (VIOLACEAE)

THE HEART-SHAPED LEAVES and dainty flowers of the dog-violet, *Viola riviniana*, can be seen in Morris's fabric *Violet and Columbine*. Among the lines in his epic poem *The Earthly Paradise* are:

And round her shapely head
A garland of dog-violet
And wind-flowers meetly had she set

Woodlands and hedge banks in spring and early summer are often sprinkled with the blue-violet flowers of the dog-violet. With its five unequal petals and heart-shaped leaves, this delicate-looking plant thrives on a wide range of soils, in woods and rocky areas, on heath and grassland. In the wild, clumps can reach nearly 1m (3ft) across. The term 'dog' implies a lower value and,

for this violet, it denotes that it has no scent.

Adaptable and easy to grow, this violet is excellent for naturalizing below a hedge or in a woodland garden. It is low and creeping, with a height of around 20cm (8in), and makes good ground cover for a shady border.

It may be readily increased by division or removal of pieces (with leaves, stems and roots) from the main clump after flowering. The separated clumps need watering until established. Plants can also be raised from seed sown in late summer, pricked out and grown on in a bedding-plant tray. A cold frame can be used to protect the seedlings over winter. Dog-violet flowers attract bumblebees, bee flies and hoverflies.

Heartsease, *Viola tricolor*, traditionally associated with love, was used by Morris in

one of his designs for the armoury and tapestry room at St James's Palace, which the Firm was commissioned to decorate in 1866. The flowers grew in the garden at Kelmscott Manor and Morris said that he found them 'beautiful'.

Popularly known as a pansy, botanically, heartsease is a *Viola* (in gardens, pansies are distinguished from violets by their face-like flowers). This annual or short-lived perennial, the ancestor of all modern garden pansies, has delicate petals varying from yellow and purple to white. A yellow spot in the centre of the flower guides pollinating bumblebees and other long-tongued insects to the entrance of the spur, where they find the nectar.

The heartsease's extraordinarily long flowering period – from mid-winter to the end of autumn – makes it an ideal addition to any rock garden or sunny bank. It will often turn up in a garden of its own volition and it is just as easy to cultivate as the garden pansies.

Grown among other plants, the wild pansy may be drawn up to a height of 45cm (18in), but it remains more compact in sun. Because of its straggly habit, it is more readily accommodated in borders than in the formality of a container.

Seeds sown in late summer after collection, or in spring, will germinate readily in a cold frame or unheated greenhouse. They germinate well on gravel drives and, as with other violets, in the wild their seed is distributed by ants. Pricked out into a bedding-plant tray, the seedlings can be held over winter in cold frames for early spring planting. Cuttings can be taken in late summer to be propagated in a free-draining compost, away from direct sun.

ABOVE Violet and Columbine, *hand-loomed wool fabric, 1883. The violets and aquilegia in this pattern are so true to life that May Morris, in her biography of her father, said:* 'Violet and Columbine *is a bowery sort of pattern, sweet and soft in colour, realistic . . .'*

OPPOSITE Viola riviniana

The wild pansy cross-pollinates freely with modern pansies; if both are grown, hybrid seedlings can soon arise. The flowers attract both bumble- and honeybees, soldier beetles and, occasionally, butterflies.

The crossing of violets to produce violas and pansies started early in the nineteenth century when cultivated strains of *Viola tricolor* were crossed and back-crossed with other pansies and the horned violet. In addition to the hundreds of modern cultivars, there are many different wild species, not to mention their several different forms and many natural hybrids.

The faces and petals of some modern hybrids are so large that it is hard to imagine that they are related to the original wild species. Violet flowers have a lower lip as a landing stage and nectar is secreted from two out-growing stamens, collecting at the bottom of the spur. However, it is often impossible for bees to get a sure footing on the larger petals of many of the new cultivars, so they cannot access the nectar.

153

CHRONOLOGY

1834
24 March: William Morris is born at Elm House in Walthamstow, Essex, to William and Emma Morris.

1840
The family takes a lease on Woodford Hall on the fringe of Epping Forest.

1847
Morris's father dies.

1848
In February, Morris begins his first term at Marlborough College, Wiltshire. Morris's widowed mother, Emma, moves the family to Water House, Walthamstow, now the William Morris Gallery.

1851
After a student rebellion at Marlborough, Morris is withdrawn and studies with the Revd Frederick Guy in Walthamstow.

1853
Morris enters Exeter College, Oxford, and meets Edward Burne-Jones. He is introduced to the writing of John Ruskin and particularly influenced by his *Stones of Venice*.

1854
Morris visits France with Burne-Jones and tours the cathedrals of Amiens, Chartres and Rouen.

1855
Morris inherits an annual income of over £740. He makes a second tour of churches and cathedrals of northern France.

1856
Morris is articled to architect G.E. Street at his Oxford office, where he meets Philip Webb. Street's office transfers to London and Morris and Burne-Jones take rooms in Bloomsbury.

1857
Morris paints frescoes with an Arthurian legend theme in the Oxford Union debating hall with Dante Gabriel Rossetti, Edward Burne-Jones, Val Prinsep, Arthur Hughes and others. He meets his future wife, Jane Burden.

1858
Morris's first volume of poetry, *The Defence of Guenevere*, is published at Morris's own expense.

1859
After a year's engagement, Morris marries Jane Burden on 26 April; they honeymoon in Bruges and Paris, and on the Rhine. Building starts on the Red House, which Morris designed with Philip Webb, and its garden at Bexleyheath, Kent.

1860
The Morrises move into the Red House.

1861
Jane (Jenny) Morris is born on 17 January. Morris, Marshall, Faulkner and Co., 'the Firm', is established in Red Lion Square, London, to make well-designed furniture, wallpaper, fabrics and other household items.

1862
Mary (May) Morris is born on 25 March. Morris designs his first wallpaper, *Trellis*. The Firm wins two medals of commendation at the International Exhibition in South Kensington.

1865
Morris, Jane and their two young daughters leave the Red House and move with the Firm, which vacates Red Lion Square, to 26 Queen Square, Bloomsbury, 'living above the shop'.

1867
Morris's *The Life and Death of Jason* is published.

1868
Parts I and II of Morris's *The Earthly Paradise* is published in April. Morris begins studying the Icelandic language.

1869
Part III of *The Earthly Paradise* is published.

1870
Part IV of *The Earthly Paradise* is published, as is *Volsunga Saga: The Story of the Volsungs and Niblungs*, translated by Eiríkir Magnússon and Morris.

1871
Morris and Rossetti acquire a joint tenancy lease of Kelmscott Manor, Oxfordshire, despite Rossetti's affair with Jane Morris. Morris goes on his first expedition to Iceland.

1872
Love is Enough is published. The family move after nearly seven years at Queen Square to Horrington House, Chiswick. Morris is among the first to produce designs for the newly established Royal School of Needlework. Rossetti suffers a breakdown.

1873
Morris makes a second trip to Iceland, and travels to Siena and Florence with Burne-Jones.

1874
Rossetti gives up his share of Kelmscott Manor. Morris and his family travel to Belgium.

1875
Morris reorganizes the Firm under his sole ownership, re-naming it Morris & Co. He begins a collaboration with Thomas Wardle.

1876
Dated 1877, *The Story of Sigurd the Volsung and the Fall of the Niblungs* is published.

1877
With Philip Webb, Morris founds the Society for the Protection of Ancient Buildings. He is offered the Chair of Poetry at Oxford University, but refuses it. He delivers his first public lecture, 'The Decorative Arts'. Morris & Co. showrooms open in Oxford Street.

1878
Morris acquires a lease on a house with river frontage at Hammersmith. He renames it Kelmscott House.

1880
Morris becomes treasurer of the National Liberal League. *The Architect* publishes a summary of his lecture 'Making the Best of It'.

1881
Morris acquires Merton Abbey workshops on the Wandle River, Surrey, and moves Morris & Co. there from London.

1882
A collection of Morris's lectures, *Hope and Fears for Art*, is published. Rossetti dies.

1883
Morris joins the Democratic Federation.

1884
Morris founds the Socialist League.

1885
The first issue of the Socialist League's journal, *The Commonweal*, is published.

1886
Morris visits Ireland and Scotland, giving speeches for the Socialist League. Serialization of his *A Dream of John Ball* begins in *The Commonweal*.

1887
The Odyssey of Homer Done into English Verse, translated by Morris, is published.

1890
The Hammersmith branch of the Socialist League severs connection with the League and is renamed the Hammersmith Socialist Society.

1891
Morris establishes the Kelmscott Press in a building near Kelmscott House, and publishes *News from Nowhere*. He becomes president of the Arts and Crafts Exhibition Society.

1892
Morris is elected master of the Art Workers' Guild.

1894
Morris's mother dies.

1896
The Kelmscott Press edition of *The Works of Geoffrey Chaucer* is published. Morris dies aged 62 on 3 October at Kelmscott House, Hammersmith, and is buried at Kelmscott in Oxfordshire.

1898
Burne-Jones dies.

SELECT BIBLIOGRAPHY

Adams, Steven, *The Arts & Crafts Movement*, Jerome Goldstein Press, London, 1996.

Anscombe, Isabelle, *Arts and Crafts Style*, Phaidon, Oxford, 1991.

Banham, Joanna and Jennifer Harris, (eds), *William Morris and the Middle Ages*, University Press, Manchester and Dover, N.H., 1984.

Baker, Derek W., *The Flowers of William Morris*, Barn Elms, London, 1996.

Batey, Mavis ed. and M. Tooley, *Gertrude Jekyll – Essays on the Life of a Working Amateur*, Michaelmas Books, London, 1995

Batey, Mavis, *Oxford Gardens*, Scolar Press, Aldershot, 1982.

Burne-Jones, Georgiana, *Memorials of Edward Burne-Jones*, Lund Humphries, London, 1993.

Bryson, John (ed.), *Dante Gabriel Rossetti and Jane Morris: their Correspondence*, Clarendon Press, Oxford, 1976.

Compton-Rickett, Arthur, *History of English Literature*, Jack, London, 1918.

Coote, Stephen, *William Morris: his Life and Work*, Garamond, London, 1990.

Cumming, Elizabeth and Wendy Kaplan, *The Arts and Crafts Movement*, Thames and Hudson, New York, 1991.

The Design Council, *William Morris & Kelmscott*, The Design Council, London, 1981.

Dore, Helen, *William Morris*, Pyramid, London, 1990.

Doughty, Oswald, *A Victorian Romantic: Dante Gabriel Rossetti*, Oxford University Press, Oxford, 1960.

Doughty, Oswald and John Robert Wahl (eds), *The Letters of Dante Gabriel Rossetti to his Publisher, F.S. Ellis*, 4 vols,. Oxford University Press, 1965-7.

Elliot, Brent, *Victorian Gardens*, Batsford, London, 1990.

Festing, Sally, *Gertrude Jekyll*, Viking, London/New York, 1991.

Fleming, Gordon H., *That Ne'er Shall Meet Again: Rossetti, Millais, Hunt*, Michael Joseph, London, 1971.

Fleming, Laurence and Alan Gore, *The English Garden*, London, Michael Joseph, 1979.

Gaunt, William, *The Pre-Raphaelite Tragedy*, Sphere Books Ltd, London, 1975.

Haslam, Malcolm, *Arts & Crafts: A Buyer's Guide*, Macdonald Orbis, London, 1985.

Henderson, Philip (ed.), *The Letters of William Morris to his Family and Friends*, Longmans, Green & Co., London/New York, 1950.

Henderson, Philip, *William Morris: His Life, Work and Friends*, Thames and Hudson, London, 1967.

Hitchmough, Wendy, *Arts and Crafts Gardens*, Pavilion Books, London, and Rizzoli International, New York, 1997.

Jekyll, Gertrude and Lawrence Weaver, *Arts and Crafts Gardens in Country Life*, originally published 1912, republished Antique Collectors Club, Wappingers Falls, NY, 1997.

Lago, Mary (ed.), *Burne-Jones Talking*, University of Missouri Press. Columbia, MO, 1981, and John Murray, London, 1982.

MacCarthy, Fiona, *William Morris: A Life for Our Time*, Faber and Faber, London, 1994.

Macgregor, Jessie, *Gardens of Celebrities and Celebrated Gardens*, Hutchinson, London, 1918.

Mackail, J.W., *The Life of William Morris*, originally published Longmans, Green & Co., London, 1899, republished Dover Publications, Inc., New York, 1995.

Marsh, Jan, *Pre-Raphaelite Women: Images of Feminity in Pre-Raphaelite Art*, Weidenfeld & Nicolson, London, 1987.

Miele, Chris (ed.), *William Morris on Architecture*, Sheffield Academic, Sheffield 1996.

Naylor, Gillian (ed.), *William Morris by Himself: Designs and Writings*, Macdonald and Orbis, London, 1988.

Naylor, Gillian, *The Arts and Crafts Movement: A Study of its Sources, Ideals and Influence on Design Theory*, MIT Press, Cambridge, Mass, 1971.

Parry, Linda (ed.), *William Morris*, Philip Wilson, London, 1996.

Poulson, Christine (ed.), *William Morris on Art and Design*, Sheffield Academic, Sheffield, 1996.

Rodgers, David, in association with the William Morris Society, *William Morris at Home*, Ebury Press, London, 1996.

Rossetti, William Michael, *The Diary of W. M. Rossetti 1870–1873*, Clarendon Press, Oxford, 1977.

Salmon, Nicholas with Derek Baker, *The William Morris Chronology*, Thoemmes Press, Bristol, 1996.

Sedding, John D., *Art and Handicraft*, Kegan Paul, Trench, Trubner & Co. Ltd, London, 1893.

Tames, Richard, *William Morris Lifelines 3*, Shire Publications Ltd, Princes Risborough, 1996.

Thompson, Paul, *The Work of William Morris*, Heinemann, London, 1967, and Oxford University Press, New York, 1991.

Vallance, Aymer, *William Morris: his Art, his Writing and his Public Life*, first published George Bell and Sons, London, 1897, republished Studio Editions Ltd, London, 1995.

INDEX

ACKNOWLEDGMENTS

AUTHORS' ACKNOWLEDGMENTS
We must first acknowledge a debt of gratitude to Mavis Batey, President of the Garden History Society, for providing us with information, checking the manuscript and, most of all, giving encouragement. We are extremely grateful to the many people who have contributed to this project. Space does not allow us to name them all but we thank especially Anthony Mockler, Arthur MacGregor (the Director of the Society of Antiquaries, who own Kelmscott Manor), and Sir Patrick Cormack, MP. We also thank our associates at Flora-for-Fauna, Dr John Marsden and Professor Chris Humphries at the Natural History Museum, and also Rosmarie Rees and Michael Sadka, who are compiling the Flora-for-Fauna Postcode Plants Database at the Natural History Museum. We must also convey gratitude to the following for their advice, technical expertise and support: Gina Douglas of the Linnean Society, the Hon. Miriam Rothschild, Professor John Parker of Cambridge University Botanic Garden, Dr Clive Stace and other members of the Botanical Society of the British Isles. Many thanks to Norah Gillow of the William Morris Gallery, Walthamstow, George Carter, Barry Delves of Hatchards, Derek Baker and David Rodgers of the William Morris Society. Thanks also go to Phillip Venning, secretary of the Society for the Protection of Ancient Buildings, and Ted Hollamby, who has lived in and preserved the Red House since 1952. And, of course, Professor William Stearn. We especially thank Priya Nithianandan, whose energy keeps Flora-for-Fauna going at the Linnean Society, and we thank *fff*'s stalwart supporters: English Nature, the Royal Botanic Gardens Kew, the Natural History Museum and the RSPCA. We are also indebted to Sir Roy Strong.

Most of all, we thank Antony Little, whose idea it was to write a book on William Morris's enthusiasm for England's plant heritage. And we also thank his companies, Osborne & Little and Liberty Furnishing Fabrics, who generously supported the research and illustrations for this book.

PUBLISHERS' ACKNOWLEDGMENTS
The Publishers would like to thank the following for their help in producing this book: Alison Freegard, Clare Pickering, Celia Levett, and Ann Barratt for the index.
Editors: Kirsty Brackenridge and Anne Askwith
Designers: David Fordham and Sarah Pickering
Picture Research: Sue Gladstone
Picture Editor: Anne Fraser
Editorial Director: Erica Hunningher
Art Director: Caroline Hillier

PHOTOGRAPHIC ACKNOWLEDGMENTS
For permission to reproduce the paintings and photographs, and for supplying photographs, the Publishers thank those listed below.
(L=left, R=right, A=above, B=below, C=centre)
A–Z Botanical Collection Ltd/Helmut Partsch 147R/A. Bragagnolo 150L; **Gillian Beckett** 115, 116AR, 129L, 140, 146; **Birmingham Museums and Art Gallery** 129R; **Bodleian Library, Oxford** 10R (MS Douce 195, Folio 6r), 54 (MS Eng.misc.d.268); **Bridgeman Art Library** 32L (Ruskin Museum, Coniston), 33 (Ashmolean Museum, Oxford), 47 (Birmingham Museums and Art Gallery), 51 (The Stapleton Collection), 128, 151; **By permission of the British Library** 10L (MS Harley 4431, Folio 376), 34 (MS Harley 4425, Folio 14v.); **Jonathan Buckley** 2, 8, 23, 24–5, 29, 42, 43, 44, 45, 70, 76–7, 124L; **Canning Press** 52L, 53, 55L, 58, 93, 94; **Bruce Coleman Limited**/R. Glover 97/Dr Eckart Pott 98A, 122L, 126R/ Kim Taylor 99A, 139L, 143R/Uwe Walz 101R/ Norbert Schwirtz 106A/ Jane Burton 106B/Hans Reinhard 107, 111, 119, 141B/Erwin & Peggy Bauer 110L/Geoff Doré 113/Wayne Lankinen 114/George McCarthy 117, 132, 150R/ Andy Purcell 121L, 126L/Jules Cowan 123R/P. Clement 134/ Colin Varndell 138L/Jens Rydell 142L/Werner Layer 145R/Sir Jeremy Grayson 152; **Country Life Picture Library** 1, 52R, 55R, 56R, 57L, 86AL, 89; **Delaware Art Museum** 59 (Samuel and Mary R. Bancroft Memorial, 1935); **Chris Donaghue, The Oxford Photo Library** 30, 31; **R. W. Ellis** 102; **Mary Evans Picture Library** 46; **Flora-for-Fauna** 104A; **Andrew N. Gagg's PHOTO FLORA** 149; **Gravetye Manor, West Sussex** 86AR; **Sonia Halliday Photographs** 82; **Hammersmith & Fulham Archives and Local History Centre** 36, 68, 69, 71, 85; **Andrew Lawson** 88, 91; **Marlborough College** 28R; **Merton Library Service** 77B, 78; **William Morris Gallery, Walthamstow, London** 5, 11R, 12, 14, 27, 28L, 39, 57R, 67, 75, 81, 83, 84, 112; **William Morris Society, London** 17, 62, 64, 112; **By courtesy of the National Portrait Gallery, London** 32R, 41; **The National Trust, Wightwick Manor** 6 (photo Cliff Gutteridge); **NHPA**/E.A. Janes 26, 101L/Matt Bain 118/Laurie Campbell 125R, 136R; © **Crown copyright. RCHME** 56L; **John Simmons** 108, 131, 137L; **The Society of Antiquaries, London** 105, 135; © **Tate Gallery, London, 1998** 37, 123L, 130–131; **V&A Picture Library** endpapers, 18, 20–21 (photo R.Davis), 38, 40, 48–9, 50, 61, 63, 66, 72 (John Dreyfus), 73, 74, 77A, 79, 98B, 99B, 100, 103, 104B, 109, 110R, 116AL, 116BR, 120, 121R, 122R, 124–5C, 127, 133, 136L, 137R, 138R, 139R, 141A, 142–143C, 144–5, 147L, 148, 153

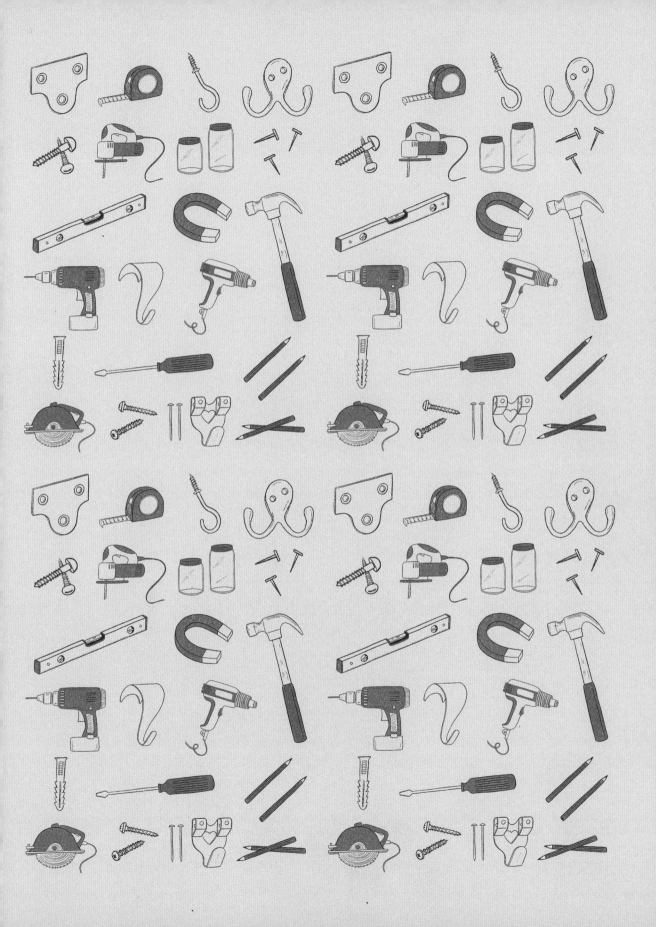